"Modern marketing is abo and data-driven strategies. As a former marketing director, Corneliu has always been convinced, ahead of many others, by the importance of marketing effectiveness and the need to leverage data to better allocate resources, better assess ROI and finally make better business decisions. I always suggested him to write a book to share his know-how and his very concrete experience on that topic. Phronesis marketing is a must have and timely book, in our fast changing, complex and digitalized environment". **Gilles Bogaert**, CEO Pernod Ricard EMEA-LATAM

"I am utterly delighted by how good - and how necessary - this book is. You are a David Ogilvy for the client side!" **Rory Sutherland**, Vice-Chairman Ogilvy UK, Author of "Alchemy: The Surprising Power Of Ideas That Don't Make Sense"

"Corneliu, as seasoned marketer in the spirits industry, offers here a review and critique of the various marketing theories that will prompt you to step back and revisit your fundamentals, before offering a new method of driving Marketing effectiveness. A most useful read !" **Cyril Camus**, President, Camus Wines and Spirits

"Vilsan is that rare thing, a CMO with decades of practical experience who has also found time to study all the latest theories **and** now write a book about how theory and practice relate to each other." **Paul Feldwick**, author of *The Anatomy of Humbug*

"The essence of the book is practical wisdom, informing the reader of the available range of tools and theories that underpin marketing, highlighting them with case studies, and advocating a blended approach to achieving success." **Ray Poynter**, Managing Director of The Future Place, Founder of NewMR, Fellow of the MRS, author of The Handbook of Online and Social Media Research

"Half the money I spend on advertising is wasted; the trouble is I don't know which half" – remember that famous quote from John Wanamaker? Well, sadly, despite the rise of intelligent digital techniques, advanced marketing automation and the explosion of the number of advertising channels, I believe this quote is still valid today to many advertisers out there. What they are missing is a clear review and understanding of the key principles of marketing and advertising. And that's what Corneliu's book will bring you and will help you make the right choices moving forward." **Philippe Dominois**, Co-Founder & CEO Abintus Consulting

PHRONESIS MARKETING

Reconciling Science with Art to Deliver Real-life
Strategies, from International Brands to Craft

CORNELIU VILSAN

Archway Publishing books may be ordered through booksellers or by contacting:

Archway Publishing
1663 Liberty Drive
Bloomington, IN 47403
www.archwaypublishing.com
844-669-3957

ISBN: 978-1-4808-9665-9 (sc)
ISBN: 978-1-4808-9666-6 (hc)
ISBN: 978-1-4808-9667-3 (e)

Library of Congress Control Number: 2020918405

Print information available on the last page.

Archway Publishing rev. date: 12/04/2020

CONTENTS

ACKNOWLEDGMENTS

To my wife, Dacia, who accompanied me for 14 years all over the globe, from Romania to the US, to Switzerland, to Croatia, to Hungary, and finally to France, where I wrote this book.

To my beloved daughter, Fabiana, who helped me write the digital section of the book and reviewed all material.

Having worked in marketing for nearly two decades, either directly as a Marketing Manager, Business Development Director, or Chief Marketing Officer, or indirectly as a Country Manager or Managing Director, I have encountered hundreds of theories, concepts, and models. A full list of books that inspired me can be found at the end of the book. Other inspirations came from my day-to-day work. The key theory of Phronesis marketing was inspired by Prof. Bent Flyvbjerg; it was developed for social sciences but focused on political science. I have adapted Prof. Flyvbjerg's model for marketing, and it is duly acknowledged as such.

Chapter 1, dedicated to the history of advertising, was greatly inspired by Paul Feldwick's book *The Anatomy of Humbug - How to Think Differently about Advertising*, a book that I think every marketer should read.

In addition to the businesses featured in the case studies, the ownership of copyright, intellectual property, and trademarks of the following companies and brands (listed alphabetically) are acknowledged: Absolut Vodka, Amazon, American Express, Aperol, AT&T, Ayala, Ballantine's, Boondocks, Budweiser, Campari, Captain Morgan, Carlsberg, Casamigos, Chivas Regal, Cîroc, Coca Cola, Corsair's, Diageo, DeLeon, Disney, Domino's, DuPont, Facebook, Fentimans, Fever Tree, General Electric, General Foods, Glenfiddich, Google, Gordon's, Gucci, Haig Club, Harley Davidson, Heineken, Home Depot, Innocent, Instagram, Jack Daniels, Jägermeister, Jameson, Jim Beam, Johnnie Walker, Jose Cuervo, J&B, Kylie Cosmetics, LinkedIn, Macallan, Mailchimp, Marc Jacobs, Martini, McKinsey, Microsoft, Monkey 47, Netflix, Nielsen, Orange, Pernod Ricard, Pfizer, Pointlogic, Procter and Gamble, Puerto de Indias, Ricard, Seagram, Schweppes, Sipsmith, Smirnoff, Starbucks, Starward, Stella McCartney, The Glenlivet, Tito's Vodka, Tom Ford, Tuborg, Twitter, Uber, Unilever, Walmart, YouTube, 3M.

INTRODUCTION

It was a hot sunny day in June of 2019, in the South of France, in the midst of the Cannes Lions international festival of creativity, that I had the chance to meet and listen to Rory Sutherland, one of the most erudite advertising professionals, who was the creative director for over 20 years and is now the vice-chairman of Ogilvy. He was speaking at a company event and recommended a book by Bent Flyvbjerg [18], now professor and chair at Oxford University, and my source of inspiration for this book.

Prof Flyvbjerg grounds much of his work on social science based on a contemporary interpretation of the Aristotelian concept of *phronesis* (ancient Greek: φρόνησῐς, romanized: *phrónēsis*), translated into French as *sagacité* and in English as *practical wisdom* or *prudence*. Prudence was a moral dimension in ancient times, together with temperance, justice, and courage, that was forgotten in the modern world. "Phronesis goes beyond analytical, scientific knowledge (episteme), and technical knowledge or know-how (techne), and involves judgments and decisions made in the manner of a virtuoso social and political actor".[18] Prof Flyvbjerg's assumption is that we can use phronesis in response to the 'science wars' between natural science and social science. It occurred to me that we can use phronesis as well to address the current marketing crisis by reconciling conflicting advertising theories, that all have their respective strengths and weaknesses, and which are described in further detail in Chapter 1. Just as the creativity theories in advertising have not contributed much to explanatory and predictive theory, neither have the rational persuasion theories contributed to the reflexive analysis of values and interests, all of which are prerequisites for the development of a successful marketing strategy and are at the core of phronesis. More on this in Chapter 5.

This book is addressed to those who do not think they already know everything about advertising: people working in advertising as well as advertising clients, senior marketing practitioners, and others who make informed marketing decisions and budget allocations, conduct market research, analyze data, and are constantly adapting their marketing strategies to the ever-changing business environment to deliver the best results.

If you are a small business owner with the ambition of becoming a big business, or a senior marketer in a bigger organization, this book is for you. It will help you either start from scratch or give you new ideas on how to improve your marketing strategy and its implementation to deliver long-term profitable results.

The business context has become tougher in recent years, especially after the COVID-19 crisis, and the environment in which advertising operates has changed: companies are under even rising pressure to increase their turnover and profits ahead of the industry average; fight for distribution, for overall margin and margin per unit sold, for cash targets and for consumer share of mind which, with an ever-increasing choice of touchpoints, becomes ever harder to achieve. Unfortunately, for more than a decade, marketing, as an organizational function, has been downgraded from its strategic role to a marginalized tactical and sales support department.

Consumers, too, have changed: they are more cynical about the constant flux of marketing messages coming to them from every channel. And their loyalty to the brands has eroded as they see more products as commodities distinguished only by price, while advertisers focus more on short term results and less on long term brand building.

The first aim of this book is to help marketing re-capture its strategic importance within the organization by going back to the basics, with a practical set of tools and case studies, to create results that can be measured, analyzed, and replicated.

Before we start, let's clarify what we mean when we say marketing, a term that is used so commonly in the business world that it has come to be known as anything from chatter at the grocery store to million-dollar ads at the Super Bowl. In this book, we use the term to describe the sum of **strategic planning** (defining markets, allocating resources among brands and markets, defining the consumer segments within the markets, defining and quantifying the needs of the consumer segments within the markets, understanding competitor value positioning and determining the value proposition to meet those needs) and **value delivery** (communicating those value propositions within the organization and playing an appropriate part in delivering them – defining objectives, strategies & value propositions, and monitoring the value actually delivered).

There are lots of books about marketing, but there are not so many written by people that implemented marketing strategically for various brands. And I am proud to have an unbeatable record of producing reliable results for more than 20 years, across multiple geographies, organizations, and industries. Unfortunately, very often the people most highly regarded in marketing are not those with the best record of creating success, but the 'gurus', who most likely have little marketing education or experience to speak of, but fascinate audiences with what's coming next and are never held accountable for the accuracy of their predictions, unless, of course, they happen to be right. As I will explain in Chapter 5, it is impossible to achieve marketing excellence without education and experience.

There are very few strategic marketing books in the market that deal with resource allocation among different countries or regions across the globe, and thus **the second aim** of this book is to fill in this noticeable gap. I have amassed and distilled thoughts and learnings I have written down over my long career as a senior executive and blended them with ideas that I have borrowed from people much smarter than myself, whom I mention in the Bibliography (which functions also as an endnotes section) and throughout the text.

Most marketing books are written either by academics or by advertising professionals. You might argue that academics use too many theoretical models and do not have enough practical experience developing real marketing strategies, brand plans, and then actually implementing them. In other words, they do not have skin in the game, they are not held accountable if their theories do not work in practice or if their theories are not implementable in real life. On the other hand, advertising professionals believe that success is not dependent on the quality of the advertising they produce to generate profits to their customers both in the short and long term, so long as it achieves the goal of bringing new clients or customers to the door. They get lost in the numbers so much that they lose confidence in the importance of creativity. They follow the money and under-prioritize creativity and creative talent in favor of technology and data, which may drive results in the short term, however it does nothing for long-term brand recognition and scalable growth.

The procurement-driven view of marketing shared by many media agencies has resulted in downward pressure on agency fees, lowering the salaries of younger recruits, and reducing the number of senior people in the organization. This *juniorization* trend had led to a decrease in expertise, insomuch that clients no longer benefit from the experience of senior practitioner advisers that might help them navigate through the complexities of the media universe. This job is now provided by consultancies.

There is no clear winner in the duel between creativity and science when it comes to the marketing industry. In fact, it's all about a power struggle. In the words of Paul Feldwick [1]: *theories of how advertising works, however implicit, have an impact on power relations within the agency, and between the agency and the client. A theory that is based on intuition and taste will privilege the creative department; a theory that is based on psychological insight may give power to the planning department; a theory based on measurement of message recall gives authority to the researchers and thus to the client.*[1]

The problematic consequence of this approach is that the tactical, short-term nature of digital advertising has taken precedence over the long-term, strategic belief in brand-building advertising. Unfortunately, the ad industry's complacency and, at times, even complicity in the online ad fraud business and privacy abuse, together with the downward pressure on remuneration, especially after the 2009 crisis, has turned off a lot of young creative talent from joining their ranks.

Ad fraud is everywhere:

- Malware creates billions of fraudulent ad impressions
- What we think are human followers can be actually bots
- Likes and shares may not actually exist or can be manipulated
- Apps can show fake downloads and even report fake sales

Fraudsters make large amounts of money by playing the ad tech ecosystem, always one step ahead of the average consumer and even advertiser. Kevin Frisch, the former head of performance marketing and CRM at Uber, said: "We turned off 2/3 of our ad spend, we turned off 100 million of annual spend out of 150, and basically saw no change [24].

According to the World Federation of Advertisers, by 2025 ad fraud may be the second-largest source of criminal revenue in the world, after drug trafficking [25].

Bob Hoffman describes brilliantly what happened: *The decade we have just experienced was expected to be one of the most fruitful and productive in the history of advertising. We had amazing new tools and amazing new media that we never had before. Our ability to personalize advertising and reach consumers "one-to-one" was sure to make advertising more relevant, timelier, and more likable. Our ability to listen to consumer conversations through social media and react quickly couldn't help but connect brands more closely with their customers. People were going to go online and join the conversation about our brands and start their own conversations and these conversations would grow and it would not cost advertisers a penny on the dollar. It all sounded so wonderful.* [22]

Except the scenario above did not come to fruition. Why is that? One of the main reasons why personalized advertising did not work is that we forgot the strategic and long-term brand equity-building role that marketing must play in order to be deemed truly successful. The marketing industry assumed the behaviors of its consumers, instead of asking them the questions they thought they knew the answer to : do consumers really share branded content, create better stories, join conversations online, co-create or feel personally engaged with these brands at a relevant scale to justify the investment?

Years and millions of dollars in advertising spend support the claim that mass advertising continues to be more effective in driving purchasing decisions and building brand reputation. Indeed, mass advertising is a form of signaling. From the brand's point of view, it demonstrates that you are an important, solid company, that can afford to advertise because you have a successful product, and that you believe in your product and its competitive advantage, otherwise you would not spend large amounts of money to support it. Consumers rely on mass advertising to tell them what is culturally acceptable and safe. *In other words, part of our purchasing calculation is not just our belief that X is an acceptable product, but our expectation that other people believe X is acceptable because they know what we know. In mass media, I know what my friends are seeing. I know that if they're watching football, they're seeing the same ads I am. Consequently, I have reasonable confidence that my friends believe that Nike makes acceptable running shoes, Ford makes acceptable pick-up trucks, and Heineken makes beer I don't have to feel weird about* [22].

The third aim of this book is to help you better understand or remind you how advertising works in real life, to give advertising clients more confidence when deciding how to invest their money in order to achieve their strategic objectives and financial results and to help them better train their marketeers and structure their organizations in order to survive in this complex consumer environment.

In recent years, consumers have increasingly come to perceive advertising as annoying, intrusive, superficial, or witless. And since online advertising is among the most disliked forms of advertising, ad-blocking apps are more and more common. But this phenomenon is not exclusive to the online advertising industry. The dislike that the average person has for the marketing profession in general is not negligible. Consumers will roll their eyes at the clichés on their television screen, count the seconds before they can skip ads on their YouTube videos, and change the radio channel at the first sign of a pesky commercial. Business professionals will similarly shrug their shoulders when asked if they believe marketing really works, often responding that they prefer a more scientific approach to revenue generation. The absence of verifiable principles in advertising is, in my opinion, the main reason why we as a profession engender so little respect in the business community. This underestimation continues to occur despite the fact that studies continue to show that user experience is significantly superior when the product is branded than when it is generic, which demonstrates that advertising creates real value.

I hope that my book will help improve the strategic position of the marketing profession within the company. Although weakened over the years by a lack of verifiable principles, the perception of marketing has improved in recent years in large part due to the work of Byron Sharp, Les Binet, Peter Field, Mark Ritson and many others I have mentioned throughout the book. I hope to add to their legacy.

So far, unfortunately, advertising has been different from any other field of study. As Bob Hoffman and Mark Ritson noted, marketeers do not respect the lessons from our history, we observe no principles, we have no connective tissue. Every generation throws away what was learned before and declares it dead. Marketing is dead. The big idea is dead. Positioning is dead. Brands are dead. The funnel is dead. Traditional media are dead. Every generation invents its own dreadful jargon that for a brief time passes for wisdom – likeonomics, engagement, conversations, storytelling, empowerment." [22]

As Thomas Barta and Patrick Barwise argue [73], modern marketers face three specific challenges:

A trust gap: marketing fails to demonstrate the financial impact of their activities and does not always predict the future with accuracy. Due to many organizations' focus on short-term results and digital advertising's ability to deliver strong evidence for short-term ROI, a large amount of investment has been redirected from long term brand building to short term 'performance marketing', and the quality of content required to keep the pace with the huge amount required is and can not be there. Producing good advertising is very hard, while codification (that links short and long term and drives salience) and creation of distinctive assets to drive Distinctiveness and Differentiation is almost forgotten.

A power gap: most of the people that determine the quality of customer experience do not report to marketing (ex: IT, trade marketing, key account managers). Marketers are not involved in strategic thinking like they used to be.

A skills gap: marketing has become so complex and changes so fast that the marketing profession has failed to keep pace with technological advances, while other departments (usually IT) took the lead in the digital transformation, without having any proper training in marketing or strategy.

Most of the concepts that you will read in this book are not new to experienced marketers and are addressing all three gaps explained above. But what this book brings to the table is an attempt at closing the gap between theory and reality, while reconciling the rational school of thought with the creative one, introducing a new concept: Phronesis Marketing. In my opinion, the Phronesis methodology is a training and learning journey that companies can implement within their organizations to achieve a higher level of understanding of how marketing and advertising work. It involves looking closely at the assumptions we make about advertising and using business cases and case studies to guide our decision-making.

This brings us to the **fourth aim** of the book: to reconcile the two contradictory models of consumer behavior that both seem to be valid - the rational or scientific model (*marketing as science*) and the emotional model (*marketing as art*). To achieve this, I will review the history of how people thought and continue to think advertising works in Chapter 1.

I will also put a lot of emphasis on the *lost art* of marketing effectiveness, or communication planning if you prefer. It is often in the interest of the new advertising actors (mainly digital gurus) to convince you that they are the only source of some sort of new wisdom on how humans think and react to advertising messages. Growth hacking has become synonymous with marketing nowadays, in many industries. Lead generation, funnels, search engine optimization, and social media have taken and continue to take up more and more share of advertising spend. While this is normal and in line with media consumption trends, there is also a limit, depending on the industry, beyond which these investments do not deliver incremental value to the business. On the contrary, too much focus on short-term results and direct marketing ROI has resulted in spending without a strategic vision. To make matters worse, the biggest online media actors refuse to adhere to the same standards of third-party verification that other media adhere to: you do not know how much competition is spending on their platforms. When you advertise on their sites you cannot verify how many people you are reaching and how long you are reaching them for. More on this in Chapter 6.

Last but certainly not least, to my knowledge, there is no book about marketing spirits (at least not on a strategic level). This is an industry that I am all too familiar with, as I have developed and executed marketing strategies for spirits for the majority of my career. With this book, I hope to begin a much-needed theoretical and practical conversation surrounding the marketing of alcoholic beverages.

There is no marketing Holy Grail. Unfortunately, if it was the Grail you were looking for when you picked up this book or any marketing book for that matter, you will not find it. Any agency that promises instant results that will both deliver measurable ROI within months and benefit your brand's long-term objectives is either lying or unaware of the falsities it is spreading. A successful marketing strategy has always been and continues to be about mastering the fundamentals, learning from experience, and optimizing based on consumer behavior. No one form of media can achieve the marketer's dream: improving brand image, gaining market share, meeting or exceeding profit targets, and doing so in a creative way that will elicit the jealousy and admiration of your peers.

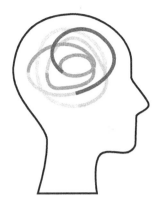

ONE

How advertising works: a short history of five major theories

I was in an executive meeting five years ago somewhere in South Africa when one of the CEOs of a big European affiliate mused: "I wonder how advertising works". At the time I was the CMO of the EMEA-LATAM region and I thought I had never heard of a more naïve question. But I was surprised I did not have a clear answer to it; it struck me afterward that maybe the question wasn't as naive as it sounded, so I decided to put together all the different theories and try to find my own interpretation of how advertising works, based on my experience. I had to answer questions like: *Should advertising be more rational or more emotional? Did the marketing world change since the invention of social media? Or does this new digital space play by remarkably similar rules to the old marketing world? Is marketing more of a science or is it pure art?* After a lot of consideration, I realized that the history of advertising helps us make sense of these dilemmas, particularly in the digital age, which seems to have come with new, unfamiliar complexities. And, to spare you the suspense, I strongly believe that, indeed, the new digital space plays by remarkably similar rules to the old marketing world, and that the traditional communication paradigm is still alive and kicking.

I gave my definition of marketing in the introduction. I will start this chapter with a definition that, in my opinion, best describes the role of the marketer: to understand consumer behavior and capitalize on the market opportunities to win in the market place by delivering value through creating memory structures or associations that drive consumers to want to choose the brand he/she is responsible for.

To understand how advertising works we need to first understand the communication and persuasion process. It starts with the strategy and advertising objective – what kind of communication effect do you want or need to achieve? While you can argue that selling is the main and most important objective of marketing communication, there are multiple sub-objectives that support this overarching goal and are often forgotten by the marketer in pursuit of short-term profitability. Below you can find a simplified model explaining the marketing communication and persuasion process:

Figure 1. Simplified model of the marketing communication and persuasion process

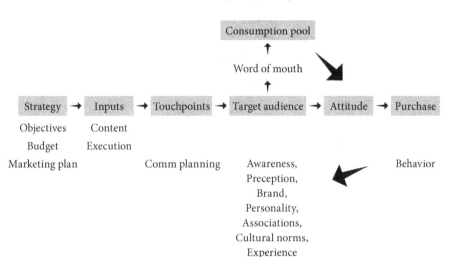

Figure 1 shows that communication does not stop at the target audience, because the target can engage in word-of-mouth communication (either verbally, in person, or via digital channels) to a wider audience that we call *consumption pool*. In practice, we know that the number one source of persuasion is not media or experience, but the recommendations of friends, family, and even strangers (be them influencers or not), making it a critical part of any successful marketing campaign.

According to Rajeev Batra, John G. Myers, and David Aaker in *Advertising Management* [35], an advertising message can have a variety of effects upon the receiver. It can:

- Create awareness, leading to a feeling of familiarity with the brand
- Communicate information about attributes on which its benefits are based

- Develop or change an image or personality, through a choice of spokesperson and various executional devices
- Associate a brand with feelings and emotions, and create a "brand personality"
- Create group norms – individuals and groups the consumers like to emulate ("to be fashionable")
- Precipitate behavior

Advertising can influence attitudes, awareness, brand personality, social norms regarding the brand, feelings associated with it, or can simply induce a purchasing decision. But let's start by looking a bit more into buyer behavior.

THE THEORY OF BUYER BEHAVIOR

Understanding consumer behavior is meant to be one of the fundamental prerequisites or characteristics of the professional marketer.

Arguably the first comprehensive theoretical structure that approached the problems of consumer behavior and brand choice using concepts borrowed from the study of behavioral science was the brainchild of Howard and Sheth, *The Theory of Buyer Behaviour*, published in 1969 [20]. It was the first attempt to put together bits and pieces of data that companies had collected in isolation to create a pattern of meaning.

In summary, Howard and Sheth describe the buying process as follows:

- In everyday life, the buyer has purchase cycles for various products, which determine how often he or she will buy these products.

- In the face of repetitive brand choices, the consumer simplifies the decision process by storing relevant information and routinizing his or her decision-making process
- It is crucial therefore to identify the elements of this decision-making process, to observe the important changes and to show how these decision elements affect search processes as well as the incorporation of information from the buyer's commercial and social environments

Figure 2

A simplified description of buyer behavior

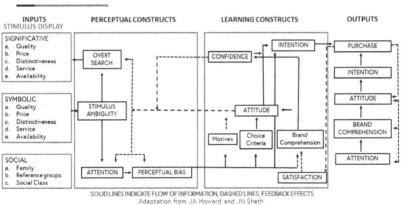

Howard and Sheth distinguish between Input (or stimulus) and output variables:

Input variables are *commercial* – either from the physical brands themselves (significative) or linguistic or pictorial representations (semiotic or symbolic): quality, price, distinctiveness, service, availability or *social stimuli* (family, reference groups, social class), the most obvious being word-of-mouth.

There are five output variables: *attention* (the buyer information intake), *brand comprehension* (the buyer's statement about his knowledge of brands), *attitude* (a buyer's verbal evaluation of a brand's potential to satisfy his needs, his description of the connotative meaning of a brand), *intention* (buyer's expectation that he will buy the brand he likes most the next time he is motivated to buy) and *purchase* of the brand.

We will not go into the minute details of this model, although we will use some of its main findings when talking about the Brand Audit in Chapter 4; I wanted to talk about it here because one thing that probably strikes you when you look at Figure 1 and especially Figure 2 is how complex they are. There are a large number of variables that can influence consumer behavior, and this is why it is so complicated to build a successful and accurate marketing theory.

In 2009, McKinsey introduced the Consumer Decision Journey (CDJ) model, after studying the purchase decisions of nearly 20,000 consumers across five industries—automobiles, skin care, insurance, consumer electronics, and mobile telecom—and three continents. Their research revealed that far from systematically narrowing their choices, like in the Funnel model, today's consumers take a much more iterative and less reductive journey of four stages: *consider, evaluate, buy,* and *enjoy-advocate-bond.* McKinsey's *active evaluation* stage updates decision-making to reflect a less linear, active process and introduces the "loyalty loop". [66] The loyalty loop, according to McKinsey, might skip the *consider* and *evaluate* stages entirely. The implications of CDJ for marketing are important: marketers need to reconsider how to allocate spending across touchpoints according to target stages in the decision journey at which consumers are best influenced, highlighting the importance of someone else's advocacy. "The coolest banner ads, best search buys, and hottest viral videos may win consideration for a brand, but if the product gets weak reviews-or, worse, isn't even discussed online—it's unlikely to survive the winnowing process." [66]

As a consequence, marketers' budgets need to consider not only the working media or *paid* media spend, but also *owned* media (like own websites and social media) and *earned* media (customer-created channels or reviews). This put a lot of pressure on increasing the non-working spend - resources allocated to people and technology to create, manage and disseminate content on online channels and to monitor or participate in them.

A recent study [58] done by Google insights team defined six cognitive biases that shape shopping behavior and influence why consumers choose one product over another:

1. Category heuristics
2. Power of now
3. Social proof
4. Scarcity bias
5. Authority bias
6. Power of free

Compared to the previous model described above, the Google's insights team model introduces two new elements that are typical to the digital age: *the power of now*, which states that the longer you have to wait for a product, the weaker the proposition becomes, and *the power of free* (a free gift with a purchase, even if unrelated, can be a powerful motivator). Both elements explain the strong proposition and attractiveness of Amazon (especially Amazon Prime), with its free same-day delivery offer and attractive prices, which helped Amazon become the most valuable company in the world in 2020.

Google's study showed as well that "even the least effective challenger, a fictional cereal brand, still managed to win 28% of shopper preference from the established favorite when it was 'supercharged' with benefits, including five-star reviews and an offer of 20% extra for free. And in the most extreme case, a fictional car insurer won 87% share of consumer preference when supercharged with advantages across all six biases." [58]. It is important to note though that Google's study was done taking into consideration only digital touchpoints (search engines, review sites, video sharing sites, portals, social media, comparison sites, forums, interest groups/clubs, retailer sites, aggregators, blogging sites, voucher/coupon sites, branded sites, publishers, noticeboards).

Advertising is full of contingencies, unintended effects, and dependent variables that all can have a big impact on the final business outcome. Because of this, even when the strategy, creative, comm planning, production, and execution departments work in perfect harmony, there is no guarantee they will deliver perfect results. But it will increase chances tremendously. To paraphrase Nicholas Taleb, my intention in this book is to defend marketing as a serious discipline, with its dual nature of logical science but also illogical artistic creativity, and to attack the marketing scientists when they deviate from their course as they do not have an understanding of critical thinking, and likewise have not proved their ability to deal with probabilities in the social sciences and they are incapable of accepting such fact. [34] On the other hand, I would like to put a limit on the role of creativity in marketing, as explained in the Marketing Effectiveness chapter.

Understanding the consumer buying decision process is becoming more difficult. In 2020, following the outbreak of COVID-19 and subsequent restrictions on physical retail, the share of purchases happening online has risen to record levels, for all categories, due to both an increase in penetration (new consumers who never bought online before) and to an increase in frequency and shopping basket size. Although the majority of purchases are and will still be made offline for many categories, the media and information that inform those purchases are increasingly online, and the complexity of potential decision-making pathways has grown considerably. [59]

Now let's focus on how marketing activities can influence attitude and therefore behavior. We will start with different advertising theories. To my knowledge, despite the ever-expanding literature on this subject, no new, ground-breaking, generally accepted principles about the nature of the brand building or consumer behavior have been discovered, as human nature has not changed fundamentally despite all the latest advances in technology. Therefore, I will stick with the classic advertising theories developed by practitioners, whilst paying tribute to some of the new theories developed mainly by start-ups, which we will find are in fact rooted in classical theories. The largest discrepancies lie not between the old and new, but between the practical and academic interpretations of marketing. Indeed, it is interesting to see that the advertising theories developed by practitioners (mainly people working in the advertising industry) differ fundamentally from those developed by the academic community. Which partly explains why marketing is in a crisis. Imagine, for example, that physicians had a different theory about how the human body works than academics: whom would you trust more? The practitioner or the academic?

Every company can gain from following in the footsteps, or simply borrowing the successful principles, that have been tried and tested by other companies, agencies, and scholars before them, and by understanding the underlying theories behind these actions. Of course, every company is different, every problem is different, every brand is different, and every context is different, but human nature has not changed fundamentally in the last 100 years and old theories work perfectly today if adapted smartly. And by using Phronesis Marketing, and creating case studies tailored to each industry, your marketing will undoubtedly become more efficient and high-quality. More on this in Chapter 7, when we talk in-depth about Phronesis Marketing.

Advertising is one field where theory and practice differ often. Some consider marketing a science, while others think it is more of an art. In recent years, the adoption of data science principles, artificial intelligence, and the large-spread emphasis on short-term ROI have driven investments in digital marketing. However, many brands that rely mainly or solely on digital marketing fail to understand how these media channels work. They buy into the idea that digital marketing allows you to input a certain budget and gain a measurable, reliable ROI every month to immediately justify their marketing investments. To paraphrase E.F. Schumacher and Paul Feldwick, marketing is not an exact science, but rather a branch of wisdom. Unlike the scientific field, where experiments can be repeated with a high degree of accuracy, advertising never finds similar conditions in the marketplace, so you cannot repeat an advertising experiment with the same expectations one would hold in a laboratory. This fact is further exacerbated by the fact that there is a lack of publicly available advertising data, as organizations are hesitant to publish their failures and only publish their successes when enough time has passed that they can be sure their competitors will not benefit from the information. The competitive nature of the advertising world continues to hinder professional advances. Furthermore, as the advertising field becomes increasingly populated by junior-level professionals, agencies cannot always build on past experience, which has sadly resulted in much less professional authority than the legal, medical, or economic professions.

It is for these reasons that I believe any serious discussion related to marketing must be grounded in an understanding of the main advertising theories that gave rise to this profession in the first place. None of these theories in isolation represents the absolute truth, but we can make use of them as a source of inspiration to apply them to each industry, product category, and business context, using a phronesis approach.

THE RATIONAL PERSUASION THEORIES

Rational persuasion theories were invented at a time when direct mail and print were the only communication channels available. They rely on a fundamental concept of advertising as selling that involves a purely rational process of persuasion, comprehension, and conviction. These theories assume decisions are rational, and that the role of advertising is to provide information and/or utility in reducing search costs (shopping time).

John Wanamaker was the first retailer to place a half-page newspaper ad in 1874. He initially wrote his own ad copy, but later hired the world's first full-time copywriter. He is best remembered for his comical, and relatable, depiction of the advertising process: "Half the money I spend on advertising is wasted; the trouble is I don't know which half."

AIDA (attributed to E St Elmo Lewis, 1898, by Strong, 1925) was an early advertising model, initially developed to train salespeople and later used to explain how advertising works. It claims that advertising is a consumer target journey through sequential stages: from **a**ttention to **i**nterest, to **d**esire, and finally **a**ction. It reflects the common belief that advertising drives sales by telling consumers things they don't know or changing their beliefs through rational persuasion. [36] AIDA introduced for the first time the concept of a hierarchy of effects, meaning that the earlier effects, being necessary preconditions, are more important.

Advertising as **"salesmanship in print"** was first introduced by John E. Kennedy, in 1904, while he was working for Lord & Thomas, the biggest American advertising agency at the time. Print was the most advanced communication channel, replacing traditional face-to-face salesmanship and complementing direct mail. Lord & Thomas differed from other agencies by claiming that 'General Publicity ' or any other advertising, should be judged against the same standards by which the salesman is judged, i.e. by the goods it is clearly proven to sell at a given cost per dollar invested in it. [40] At the beginning of the 20th century, the quality of products varied considerably as industrialization had only just begun to take hold of the American economy. *"The striving to attract attention instead of striving to positively sell goods is the basis of all advertising misunderstanding. So long as 'attracting attention' remains the aim of advertisers, so will the process of attracting it remain in the hands of advertising men who affect the literary and artistic attitude, rather than the plain logical convincing attitude of the salesman-on-paper. Because great is the temptation to be considered smart, bright, catchy, literary, artistic. There is popular applause for the writer of catchy 'General Publicity' which attracts attention even though it does not sell goods. Makers of General Publicity know they can never be held to account for definite results from that kind of copy, because nothing definite is promised through it."* [40]

Lord & Thomas had about one-third of business in direct mail and two thirds in general advertising (i.e. selling in retail stores) and were claiming that the direct mail principles applied in retail as well. They introduced the first Advertising Test, which consisted in benchmarking sales in two cities of equal size, climate and equally good media, over a four months period: one city running the current advertising copy and the other one running the Lord & Thomas *Salesmanship on paper* copy, for the same amount of Advertising budget. The results of these tests were included in the *Record of*

Results, a database of results from previous campaigns (Figure 3). Without such a *Record of Results*, they claimed, "all advertising copy and selection of mediums would be mere gambling - baseless opinion, guesswork, and experiment".

This concept was so basic and so effective and powerful that it is still used today (of course, it has evolved to include Salesmanship in other media channels). Kennedy also invented the **"reason why"** rational advertising and introduced copywriting to the marketing profession, becoming the best-paid copywriter in the world at the time. Lord & Thomas believed that the 'qualities' of the product, "claimed and proved for it in the copy, might have never been discovered in a mere 'curiosity' purchase, as a result of General Publicity". [40]

Figure 3: Lord & Thomas 'Record of Results' database

The **"scientific method"** was first introduced by Claude Hopkins in 1923. A famous quote from Claude Hopkins' book, *Scientific Advertising*[3], in fact, the very first phrase of the book, provides an excellent summary of the theory behind his method: "*The time has come when advertising has in some hands reached the status of a science. It is based on fixed principles and is reasonably exact. The causes and effects have been analyzed until they are well understood.*

The correct methods of procedure have been proven and established. We know what is more effective and we act on basic law. Advertising, once a gamble, has become, under able direction, one of the safest business ventures."

Hopkins's 17 principles were based on traced mail order responses (largely through the use of coupons):

- **Salesmanship** (the only purpose of advertising is to make sales) – a concept taken from Kennedy
- **Offer service** (ads should offer information that is wanted and required by the consumer)
- **Headlines** (create headlines for people who are interested in your offer and select those qualities that most of your readers seek)
- **Psychology** (ads are based on the knowledge of psychology, whose principles are fixed and enduring)
- **Be specific** (the weight of an argument may be multiplied by making it specific)
- **Tell your full story** (test your appealing claims and present all of them to the reader)
- **Art** (use pictures only to attract those who will provide a profit to you; do nothing to merely interest, amuse or attract)
- **Things too costly** (avoid excessively costly endeavors, like creating a trend or educating people; instead, capitalize on trends and let others do the education for you)
- **Information** (facts are the keynote for success, do your research using reams of data to find the right claims)
- **Strategy** (brand name, price, competition, dealers, distribution)

- **Use of samples** (most people want to trial a product before investing, and samples are often the cheapest way to get new customers)
- **Distribution** (start with local advertising before going national; co-promote with dealers)
- **Test campaigns** (start with a small sample before scaling up; compare ads through A/B testing)
- **Lean on dealers** (discounts and gifts could be far better spent on securing new customers)
- **Individuality** (introduce a personality in your ads, never change the tone)
- **Negative advertising** (to attack a rival is never good advertising; show your happy and attractive, healthy and successful side, not the dark and uninviting side of your business)
- **Letter writing** (test your letters – or emails – like you test your ads)

Direct response, as promoted by the scientific method, is a form of advertising where people are urged to respond directly to your advertisement, and it is based on well-funded behavioral experiments. One could argue that, in many ways, the salesmanship in print and scientific methods learnings based on direct response marketing could be easily translated to inform today's direct-response world: e-commerce and digital marketing. Indeed, Kennedy and Hopkins can be considered the fathers of direct response, A/B testing, and various other techniques in Growth Marketing. Both theories were based on the assumption that you can easily measure Return on Investment due to the direct correlation between marketing input (content, cost) and output (sales), a process that has been made both easier nowadays due to advanced tracking methodologies and harder due to wide-spread attribution errors.

The ad below provides a good example of *salesmanship in print* in practice.

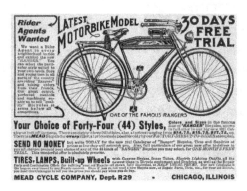

By 1923, a professor at Harvard Business School, Daniel Starch, improved the AIDA and *salesmanship in print* models by adding a new element: *memory*, that extends the previous models to explain the time lag between conviction and action when advertising does not lead to an immediate sale. Starch introduced in 1937 the famous **Starch rating**, which still exists today and treats recognition as a measure of advertising effectiveness. The Starch rating was criticized because there is no clear relationship between recognition and sales and it can be easily manipulated by showing for example attractive characters, odd images, cryptic headlines, or other attention-grabbing tricks that attract attention but do not necessarily sell the product. [18] However, the rating and its subsequent emphasis on grabbing the audience's attention worked very well in an era dominated by mass-circulation color magazines [1].

In 1924, William Townsend introduced, in association with the AIDA model, the **Purchase funnel** concept, also known as the *customer funnel, marketing funnel, sales funnel,* or *conversion funnel.* The *Purchase funnel* concept is used intensively today to guide promotional campaigns targeting different stages of the customer journey and as a basis for customer relationship management (CRM) programs and lead management campaigns.

In 1961, Rosser Reeves introduced the **USP: 'Unique Selling Proposition'** concept in response to the emergence of broadcast TV as a new marketing medium, arguing that most competing products did not really differ, and therefore advertising needs a simple sales message that can easily be remembered: *one strong claim, one strong concept.*

Reeves created a new definition of advertising: "the art of getting a USP into the heads of the most people at the lowest possible cost" that survives even today as a commonly held belief in agencies, despite the fact that it is not based on any real evidence or coherent theory [1]. Reeves created USP as part of the long-standing recognition of the idea, now called **positioning**, that a brand must differentiate itself, if possible, through tangible product attributes and then communicate it positively [41]. Reeves believed that USP made the difference between hard selling and product puffery or show windows.

Reeves also believed that to make a claim that the product does not possess, does not accurately represent the product's main attributes (a deceptive differential) or which the consumer cannot observe, merely increased the frequency with which the consumer observed its absence. He also recommended that comparisons must not be made against minor, unknown products, with little distribution, and that comparisons do not necessarily make better campaigns. "If it is true, you can say it. The way you say it is a matter of copy philosophy, or taste, or your degree of selling enthusiasm. If it is not true, you cannot say it. Think of USP not so much as something you put in your advertising, but rather as something the consumer takes out of the advertising. It is what comes through." [46]

In 1961, in a report to the Association of National Advertisers, Russell Colley introduced **DAGMAR** (Defining Advertising Goals for Measured Advertising Results), a marketing model used to establish clear objectives for an advertising campaign and measure its success. The model was expanded upon in the 90s by Solomon Dutka. DAGMAR demonstrated how attaining advertising objectives can be greatly enhanced through the use of clearly defined advertising goal-setting procedures and ongoing measurement of their achievement [60]. An advertising goal is defined as "a specific communication task, to be accomplished among a defined audience to a given degree over a designated period of time" [60]. At the goal-defining stage, the task is not how to write copy, but what needs to be said. An example of a DAGMAR objective is: "To increase - from 10% to 40% - among the 70 million homemakers who use automatic washers, the number who identify Brand 'X' with ingredient 'Y' as a low-sudsing detergent which cleans clothes better and faster than others" [60]. Agreement needs to be reached on *what needs to be said to whom,* while planning is separated, defining how money is spent on *how best to say it.*

The DAGMAR model defines the four steps of an effective advertising campaign as causing awareness, comprehension, conviction, and action. Colley specified four basic requirements for evaluating the effectiveness of an advertising campaign [60]:

- Be concrete and measurable
- Define the target audience or market
- Identify the benchmark and the degree of change expected
- Specify a period during which to accomplish the objective

In the 90s started the *Moment of truths* concept and Customer Experience Management. The idea is that consumers still want a clear brand proposition and offerings they value, but what has changed is at which touchpoints they are most open to influence and how to interact with them in the most efficient way using these digital touchpoints.

In 1989, Jan Carlzon wrote a famous book called *Moments of Truth: New Strategies for Today's Customer-Driven Economy.* [74] Carlzon turned around Scandinavian Airlines by focusing on what he later called "**moments of truth**", the various points at which people with the airline came in contact with airline customers. His insight was that, "if you really want to be business-oriented and customer-driven, you must give the responsibility not to the top management of the company, not to the middle management, but to every individual person managing those moments of truth out there in the front line." [61]

In 2005, AG Lafley, Chairman, President & CEO of Procter & Gamble, introduced the First and Second Moment of Truth. **First moment of truth** is defined as the moment when a customer is first confronted with the product, either offline or online. [62] It occurs within the first 3-7 seconds of a consumer encountering the product and it is during this time that marketers have the capability of turning a browser (physical or digital) into a buyer. [68] Procter & Gamble describe the first moment of truth as the "moment a consumer chooses a product over the other competitors offerings". [65]

Second moment of truth is when a customer purchases a product and experiences its quality as per the promise of the brand.[63] There can be multiple second moments of truth for every time the product is consumed or used [68], providing the consumer with information for future purchases and for sharing their experience with the product/service. [67]

The **Zero Moment of Truth** was coined by Google in 2011. This is when prospects recognize a need and go online to gather information regarding a potential purchase (of course, using Google most of the time, as they had 86% share of desktop research as of April 2020, according to Statista).[68] Based on Google's research, people checked 10.4 sources of information to make a decision in 2011, an increase from 5.3 sources in 2010. [63]

In conclusion: The *Rational Persuasion* theories are used even today because humans have a natural love of certainty and predictability, and because many times they actually work!

Critique of Rational Persuasion theories

Critics of the Rational Persuasion theories claim that advertising is mostly a weakly persuasive force, and consumers largely discount persuasive claims, as they know advertising is a biased message trying to sell them something. They argue that one-to-many advertising, which typically lasts a few seconds, works very differently from a salesperson's one on one interaction, which lasts much longer and can be more persuasive by adapting the conversation to what is most relevant to the customer. [36] Furthermore, they maintain that brands should focus on crafting a story as opposed to a proposition, as is the case with Jack Daniels (see case study in Chapter 5). Nobody can argue with a good story, one that is successful in grabbing the customer's attention, establishing an emotional connection, and creating a memory structure that simply cannot be achieved through rational messaging.

Some famous brands would have never been created if they had been based on the *reason why* logical thinking. For example, one might argue that the Red Bull energy drink, Jägermeister bitter, and Lagavulin single malt whisky have a taste that most people hate and that Starbucks sells coffee at ten times the price of making it at home; "non-alcoholic gin" is basically flavored water sold as an adult soft drink at five times the price of other flavored waters, and so on. These brands and many other beverage brands rely on the fact that the situation or place or social context in which we find ourselves may completely change our perception and judgment.

The scientific method is part of the direct response lineage we associate with what we used to call junk mail: ads with coupons, 800 numbers, and nowadays *buy now* buttons. Hopkins is an example of the hard sell or salesmanship school that focuses on increasing direct sales and works very well for short-term, rational messages. It is certainly a great approach to continue to apply for those in e-commerce or B2B sales. However, recent research has shown that emotional messaging generates much better results than rational messaging in terms of long-term brand building. [14, 15] Not only does advertising not always work according to traditional rational theories but, with the advance of production processes, there is very little differentiation between products' physical attributes and it is much more difficult today to sell based on attributes than it was at the beginning of the 19th century.

Jenni Romaniuk, in *Building Distinctive Brand Assets* [73], demonstrated that brand distinctiveness and consistency, rather than positioning, builds a long-term strong brand identity.

Rosser Reeves' anti-creative and anti-fluff USP theory, although often effective, could not prevent competitors from using the same USP and pricing it more attractively. Nowadays, many products in the market are no better or worse than your product, with the exception, perhaps, of their packaging. "While Reeves' style of advertising was often effective, it treated the consumer like a tasteless moron, willing to swallow any claim, no matter how senseless or shallow, like an obedient sheep. As his message spread and more agencies began to imitate his style, the advertising industry turned itself into a joke, parodied and pilloried in books, radio, movies, and television" [49]

THE GROWTH MARKETING THEORY

The *Growth Marketing* or *Growth Hacking* theory, which is basically the scientific method applied to a digital world, started in large part due to early-stage startups that needed to achieve massive growth in a short period of time at the lowest possible cost to prove they have a sustainable business model and attract investors. Similar to the move that happened when the impact of television shifted creative power from copywriters to the copywriter/art director duo, we now experience a power shift from art directors to data specialists.

New terms and KPIs have been introduced that did not exist in traditional advertising, like Pivot, Minimum Viable Product, Build-Measure-Learn, Click-Through-Rates, and Acquisition Cost, all relying exclusively on accounting, math, and metrics. A growth hacking team is made up of marketers, developers, engineers, and product managers that focus on building and engaging the user base mainly through digital channels: social media, SEO, SEM, and targeted online advertising (email, programmatic, retargeting).

The number of digital ad formats has exploded: from photos and 30' videos we now have gifs, shorter videos (1-6' or 6-15'), 360 photos and videos, canvas, IG stories, video/photo carousel, live streaming, in-stream videos and the list goes on.

Creative production needs to be optimized to target the right audience with the right content at the right cost. Content can be automatically created based on best performing ads. A wide range of assets are produced internally, in creative studios, or using freelancers, providing savings vs the agencies but putting consistency at risk.

To cope with this complexity, a version of the AIDA or Purchase Funnel model was developed by venture capitalist Dave McClure, who categorizes five distinct elements of building a successful business: **A**cquisition, **A**ctivation, **R**etention, **R**evenue and **R**eferral (*AARRR*). These elements do not necessarily follow a strict order and have many metrics associated with it (ex: *Acquisition* is measured by traffic, mentions, cost-per-click, search results, cost of acquisition, open rate, and *Revenue* is measured by Customer Lifetime Value, conversion rate, shopping cart size, and click-through revenue). [37]

Eric Ries talks about three engines that drive the growth of a startup: *Sticky Engine* (measured by *Customer Retention* and *Time since last visit*), *Virality Engine* (measured by the *Virality Coefficient*, or the number of new users that each user brings on) and the *Paid Engine* (the ultimate metric for identifying a sustainable business model, measured by *Customer Lifetime Value* and *Customer Acquisition Cost*). [38] He believes that people working in big corporations are fundamentally different from creative, disruptive entrepreneurs, the difference being that disruptive entrepreneurs thrive on speed and uncertainty. [39]

In the early days of the Web, sales were all about transactional websites, which had pretty simple conversion funnels: home page, navigate to the desired product page, enter payment information, and confirm the order. Today's funnel extends beyond the website to social networks, sharing platforms, affiliates, recommendation engines, and price-comparison sites, all measured through a tracking code (like a cookie) placed on the customer when he or she first interacts with the brand. We have Customer Data Platforms, Data warehouses, Marketing Automation Platforms and Marketing clouds. With the rise of eCommerce, companies are increasingly interested in a long funnel that begins with a Facebook or Instagram post, a tweet, a video or a link, and ends with a purchase. Online retailers need to understand what messages, distributed on which platforms, and with what frequency generate the kinds of visitors that will ultimately buy their products. Once the potential buyers are on the site, the emphasis is on maximizing the amount of products or services they purchase in a transaction.

Recent technological advances have had an immense impact on the way advertisers understand and approach consumer behavior. [1] One example of the technological change paradigm is the analysis presented by Seth Stephens-Davidowitz [11], an internet expert and former data scientist at Google, who believes that Google is a sort of "cerebroscope", a mythical device that can display a person's thoughts on a screen: what they really want, what they really do, and who they really are. It is part of a bigger trend that believes that listening or observing what consumers do or say on the internet is much more viable than asking consumers, because consumers "lie" in surveys, but "tell the truth" while searching on the internet. He uses (mostly) Google Trends, a tool released in 2009 to tell users how frequently any word or phrase has been searched in different locations and in different times, and study (mostly) the American psyche. "The power of Google data is that people tell the giant search engine things they might not tell (or admit to) anyone else", like their sex life (Stephen-Davidowitz discovered that people have less sex than what they declare), or how the Obama election changed the racist map in the US, or that places with lower education levels and lower-income levels show a higher level of anxiety, and so forth. "Digital data now shows us there is more to human society than we think we see; it might be our era's microscope or telescope – making possible important, even revolutionary insights". [11]

But the thing that surprises me the most, and which differentiates growth marketers from traditional advertisers, is the way digital actors use best practice sharing (an important part of Phronesis marketing, see Chapter 5) to share insights in regards to a myriad of technical innovations. For example, Facebook recently made plenty of changes to their platform, introducing what they call "The Power of Five" (dynamic ads, auto advanced matching, account simplification, campaign budget optimization, and automatic placements), which is basically about using machine learning to help advertisers determine optimal bidding strategies and funnel-based structure to boost performance. Facebook algorithms can now optimize your ads in real-time across placements and platforms much better than what you could achieve yourself, making testing online creatives (image, body copy, and headlines), including dynamic creatives, easier than ever. Soon after these innovations were announced by Facebook, the digital marketing community started to share best practices based on individual users' and agencies' experience, which ultimately resulted in a high rate of adoption. Even amateur advertisers that are looking to leverage Facebook advertising for their small business know the basics of Facebook advertising and conversion tracking due to the wealth of information made available by others. Instagram, a subsidiary of Facebook, is currently offering one of the lowest cost per thousand impressions (CPM) out there, and provides a variety of options for digital advertisers, constantly introducing new communication mediums through which to engage its ever-growing user base. For example, in 2016, Instagram launched Instagram Stories and quickly monetized them in 2017 to allow advertisers to interrupt their audience's scrolling to view a 15-second ad. Next, Instagram launched IGTV in 2018 to capitalize on the ever-booming market for videos, which allow brands to post and promote long-form content. Finally, Facebook has capitalized on advances in human language processing to introduce chatbots for Messenger, which can be used not only for customer support but also for advertising and re-engaging prospects. Right now, private messaging and engaging video content are the hottest trends in online communication. It's amazing how quickly these innovations are adopted, and this has a great deal to do with the knowledge sharing amongst the digital marketing community.

Growth Marketing works well in markets where consumers require a lot of information before they make expensive purchase decisions - finance, insurance, travel and tourism, transportation, restaurants, automobiles, B2B, certain retail sectors, but also with customers who are already interested in what is being sold (fashion, beauty, electronics, home appliances). Emails to existing customers who have bought before are exceptionally cost-effective in wines, books, holidays, entertainments, although volume of business is relatively small [54].

Critique of Growth Marketing Theory

As Bob Hoffman would say, "Do you think Donald Trump would have become President if The Apprentice had been a webinar?"

Engagement on social media is decreasing while the CPMs are rising. As of the writing of this book, the average Facebook CPM is about 10$ and can go up to 60$ - especially after Facebook decided to de-prioritize publisher content on its news feed, according to Adstage per Recode. The same for Google AdWords: CPM (Cost Per Thousand) & CPC (Cost Per Click) increased while CTR (Click-Through Rates) decreased.

However, the main drawback associated with digital marketing has to do with its narrowed focus on achieving short-term objectives. Many marketers expected online advertising to fulfill long-term brand building objectives and even to replace traditional advertising and PR, and this has simply not been the case. It has proven to be mostly an augmented direct response factory – electronic junk mail. Many creative departments are now run by *clickonomics* experts that create images and video content intended to generate a response as opposed to creating a brand narrative. [22] Broadcast media continues to grow in importance in both developed and developing markets, and even if the targeting accuracy of digital has improved, it does not replace the need to communicate mass-market, as Byron Sharp, Les Binet, and Peter Field have demonstrated. Nevertheless, the ways in which Television is accessed today, allowing for better targeting, is changing fast and will have implications for advertising. [1]

More recently, the Facebook and Instagram boycott by major advertisers was based on perceived inefficient efforts of Facebook to suppress hate speech in the face of increased hateful content online that are being developed.

Growth hacking produces many vanity metrics, numbers that make you feel good but are misleading, like the number of views and clicks your ad gets. We need a new understanding of how to measure progress in the digital world to accurately portray the results of these campaigns. Most marketers are collecting data to better understand the customer and then send personalized communication using Customer Relationship Management (CRM). While this approach may seem logical and even be successful in the short term, this data is generally used to send useless, annoying content and can be a huge waste of time, money, and energy for the marketing department. Data is valuable only if you actually do something useful with it as opposed to irritating potential customers by invading their inbox.

Unfortunately for data advocates, reducing advertising to a set of rules or psychological principles that could be successfully applied in a consistent way and therefore programmed or used in a machine learning program has proven unsuccessful in most of the cases. The average consumer is bombarded with thousands of marketing messages a day, so it is almost impossible to get any one noticed or remembered. Online ad fraud continues to distort the numbers and increased expectations regarding digital brand buildings have not materialized. Furthermore, you will find that brands that have achieved success in the digital world, both in terms of finances and brand awareness, relied on a variety of advertising channels and strategies as opposed to following a strict regimen of digital marketing. Few big actors out there can truly point to online as the source of their success and continued growth, though it certainly plays a large role for eCommerce businesses in particular.

Recent boycott of Facebook showed that the top 100 of Facebook's biggest advertisers (among them Home Depot, Disney, Walmart, American Express, Microsoft, Starbucks, Procter & Gamble, Unilever, Pfizer, Uber, Netflix, Domino's and AT&T) only account for just 6% of the company's annual ad revenue of 71 B$. [52] Most Facebook advertisers come from small and medium-sized businesses which can not afford traditional media or have a D2C business model that does not require traditional media. Companies like P&G and Unilever spend only about 0.5-1.3% of their total advertising budget on Facebook, according to Pathmatic and recent company corporate results [52].

Although I am not a Big Data skeptic, on the contrary, and I do believe that "we can find the needle in an increasingly larger haystack", to paraphrase Nassim Taleb, I do believe Big Data has its limitations. Sometimes it provides information that is either obvious or unnecessary, while otherwise it provides useful information that cannot be used due to GDPR regulations.

About five years ago, I conducted text analysis research by scraping hundreds of thousands of comments on social media for whisky brands in the US, trying to understand differences in brand image, predict market share movements based on different words used by consumers, and measure 'consumer sentiment'. We predicted that shares for a certain whisky brand that will remain unnamed for the purposes of data privacy will decrease because of negative sentiment following its acquisition by a Japanese company (it didn't, on the contrary) and that consumers of a famous Irish whiskey brand prefer it either neat or on the rocks (we knew that already, and it was not distinctive for that brand).

Whenever information growth outpaces our understanding of how to process it, we may need to take a step back and be more realistic of what the new technology can accomplish for us. As Nate Silver noticed, "Chris Anderson, the editor of Wired magazine, wrote in 2007 that the sheer volume of data would obviate the need for theory and even the scientific method". [57] Obviously, this did not happen, and it is unlikely to happen. Based on my experience, data-driven analysis and prediction can fail if we do not play our role in interpreting it, based on our contextual experience. Fusing human judgment and computer power can deliver amazing insights; we need models and we need to know the limitations of the models to properly use them, by being aware of the biases we introduce by trying to simplify the complex world in which we live.

While data provides valuable insights, it also creates dangerous pitfalls, namely an over-reliance on correlations. Those who work with data know that, in very large sample sizes, most data points will have statistically significant correlations, because on some level everything is related to everything else. [12] The danger is to create *false positives*, that is findings that have statistically significant confidence levels, but which are not correct. To avoid this outcome, we need both statistical techniques that can be used to improve the accuracy of correlations and contextual expertise: a deep understanding of consumer behavior and category expertise, that comes with experience. Of course, experience has its own limitations. For example, when data is random but happens to include a sequence (like tossing a coin and getting six heads in a row), we tend to over-interpret the importance of this pattern. Humans, like machines, like to find patterns and create meaning, even when it doesn't exist. [12]

Claiming that consumers are 'empowered' by recent digital innovations, which allow them to more easily compare products and prices, rests on the assumption that they were stupid in the past and have suddenly ceased to be influenced by branding. Except studies show that consumers are still buying brands and branded experiences, and private labels have not managed to conquer the world as predicted by some advertising nihilists.

On the other hand, I do not know any beverage brand that achieved success using a Growth Marketing strategy.

I will end this subchapter with Paul Feldwick's [1] list of things that haven't changed much in the last hundred years, despite the technological change, because the fundamentals of how people learn, perceive, choose, and influence each other didn't change even when television, mobile phone, and Twitter were introduced, and will not change in the foreseeable future:

- The emotional basis of decision making
- People's interest in reading text
- What makes people laugh or cry
- The desire to share opinions with others
- The need to contact someone in charge when things go wrong
- Consumers' attention span (despite wild claims to the contrary)
- Attitudes in regard to being interrupted at the wrong moment
- Buying decisions mediated by brands
- The importance of price
- The importance of Low Attention Processing in persuasion
- Interest in relevant facts when making certain purchases
- The ability of individuals over the age of 50 to read small print
- Susceptibility to sexual attractiveness
- Enjoyment of music
- Wanting to feel connected
- Appreciation of good service and wanting to feel valued as a customer

 ## THE CREATIVITY THEORY

The creativity theory maintains that creativity plays the biggest role in brand building. Advertising is a branch of wisdom, right? Or as Rory Sutherland, one of my favorite authors would put it, *the case for magic*: "while in physics the opposite of a good idea is generally a bad idea, in psychology the opposite of a good idea can be a very good idea indeed: opposites often work". "The principles of selling and behavior change are imbued with contradictions."

Many successful advertising campaigns contain no useful information about the brand. More than thirty years of experimental social psychology research done by behavioral economics researchers demonstrated that decision making is closely related to emotions, feelings, and context and there is no such thing as purely rational decision making.

Ernest Dichter, an Austrian by birth, created 'Motivation Research' in 1940. The main idea, borrowed from Freud, was that people's own motivations for their actions are normally unknown to them and are mere post-rationalizations, while the real motives are subconscious and based on emotional drives like security, status, and sex. Dichter developed and perfected the focus group (and coined the term), which permanently injected psychology into market research. He later anticipated some work of semioticians and claimed to have invented the brand image concept, although the official birth of the brand image was in 1955, when Gardner and Levy published an article in the Harvard Business Review. Dichter famously said that "What people actually spend their money on in most instances are psychological differences, illusory brand images." [69]

Another famous name in Motivation Research is Louis Cheskin, who alongside Leo Burnett, re-designed the Marlboro brand to appeal to men by using the signature, strong red color, and the chevron device, which he believed subconsciously evoke the image of a medal and thus heroic masculinity. The same chevron device helped the re-launch of Ballantine's, a Scotch whisky, in 2000.

But even creative directors have their secrets, from layout and to typography. [9] Achieving fame is very difficult or even improbable if you do not have the right assets to achieve your fame: money and creativity. And since money is scarce nowadays, your only chance to win might be to win on creativity.

James Webb Young's book, *A Technique for Producing Ideas* [13], a tiny little book written in the 1940s, with a foreword by Bill Bernbach, is still important today for creative people and for those who want to generate ideas in general. It is an illuminating description of the creative process, offering both guidance and assurance that coming up with an idea is a process, not an accident, and not pure intuition. His aim was to identify the idea-building processes that go on beneath the surface of the conscious mind and document it. "The production of ideas is just as definite a process as the production of Fords; the production of ideas runs, too, on an assembly line; in this production, the mind follows an operative technique which can be learned and controlled; its effective use is just as much a matter of practice in the technique as in any effective use of a tool".[13] Below, I will detail his technique, as it is rarely mentioned in business literature.

This *kaleidoscope* process is based on two main principles and one method. The two principles are:

- An idea is a combination of old and new concepts
- The ability to make new combinations depends on creating a habit of the mind to search for relationships

The relationships can be words as symbols for ideas (ex: *What is the one-word symbol which will best arouse the emotion with which I wish this particular advertisement to be charged?*, or *What is the relationship between the product and the target consumer?*) or relationships between facts. This habit of the mind, if cultivated, believes Webb Young, will lead to the extraction of a general principle, which in turn will suggest a new application, a new combination, and the result is an idea.

Webb Young's Idea producing method consists of five steps:

- Gather raw materials (specific to the product and the strategic target, and general knowledge about life and events)
- Let them digest inside your head
- Put the problem out of your mind as completely as you can to stimulate the unconscious, creative process
- The Idea will appear when you least expect it, be ready for it
- Submit your idea to the criticism of others, and stimulate them to add to it things you might have overlooked

James Webb Young is also famous for proposing, in *How To Become an Advertising Man* [77], five ways in which advertising works: familiarizing, reminding, spreading news, overcoming inertias, and adding a value not in the product.

I will present in Chapter 5, in the Absolut Vodka case study, the most creative campaign ever produced for a beverage brand.

Alfred Politz and his homonymous market research firm, which dominated the development and implementation of new quantitative methods for advertising research for nearly 30 years, gave us the legacy of random probability sampling shaped market research. Politz pointed out that while "purchase is the ultimate purpose of advertising, purchase behavior per se is strictly a physical activity. The effects of advertising, on the other hand, are psychological phenomena". [60]

In 1957 Pierre Martineau, in his *Motivation for Advertising* [78], observes that "modern advertising (...) is far from being just a reliance on words and logic. It is rather a fusion of many modes of human communications, including language. Advertising (...) uses layout and illustration, both photography and art; it uses color and music, even choreography and drama. Actually it also uses language in a far more expressive way than just to present rational thought. Any given ad (...) may have aesthetic appeal, entertainment value, or irrelevant but highly valuable information, as well as various psychological attractions. Besides economic self-interest, advertising leans heavily on such other psychological processes as suggestion, association, repetition, identification, fantasy, etc... so much more is going on than just a sales argument with the consumer". Martineau believes that "words more often than not play a minor role in what is actually happening". The secret of successful campaigns, we are told, is that **brand-image** campaigns communicate with the reader by establishing contact with the consumers' subconscious, with visual symbols instead of words. Visual symbols are more significant, communicate faster, are more direct, require no mental effort, and create images and moods by presenting psychological realities, which are as powerful as physical realities. According to Hoffman, brand images are "part of the cultural landscape we inhabit. They provide cultural information. When we ignore brand messages we're missing out on valuable cultural information and alienating ourselves from the Zeitgeist." [22] This puts us in danger of becoming outdated, unfashionable, or otherwise socially hapless. We become like "the kid who wears his dad's suit to his first middle school dance." In other words, in some way, brand choices send messages to others about who we are. And no one but a sociopath wants to send the wrong message." [22].

I am presenting in Chapter 5, as an example, in Jack Daniel's case study, the most powerful brand image campaign ever produced for a spirits brand.

Rosser Reeves, former chairman of the Board of Ted Bates & Co and a bright and energetic copywriter, brought a no-nonsense approach to business and warned against the egos of copywriters, which he argued caused them to value the creativity of the ad over the selling message of the product. He claimed to have reconciled USP with brand image, saying that brand image is the philosophy of a feeling, while USP is the philosophy of a claim. "What you remember of an orator – his dress, his personality, his conviction - is brand image. What he said -that is USP. Either, without the other, may be successful in itself, but the combination of the two can have overwhelming power". [46] Reeves, a great believer in consumer research, went on to establish a 'Copy Laboratory', a place where copywriters could test the efficacy of their messages. The brand personality is like pieces of a mosaic or like a bird's nest. It is made of small pieces that must be put together or assembled into one striking and memorable theme, for the public cannot carry all the individual pieces in its head.

The so-called *creative revolution* is ascribed to Bernbach and Ogilvy in the 50s. The famous **Bill Bernbach**, one of the founders and the creative geniuses behind DDB (Doyle Dane Bernbach), is seen by many as the single most influential creative force in advertising history. He used to say: "Advertising is fundamentally persuasion, and persuasion happens to be not a science, but an art. Rules are what the artist breaks; the memorable never emerged from a formula". [79] He is the one who brought grace, charm, warmth, humanity, humor, and wit but also egalitarianism to advertising, insisting on employing talent that revolutionized the ad industry. He is also credited for creating the paradoxical version of reality which most agencies live with even today: on one hand, advertising is seen as a matter of logic, facts, and salesmanship: the product, the proposition which can be debated with the client. On the other hand, the execution has to do with taste, artistry, and magic, which are not for discussion. This creates a disconnect between the rational business conduct of Segmentation, Target Audiences, Propositions, and Functional Benefits included in the creative brief, and the creatives that have nothing to do with the brief, but that might still sell nevertheless. Unless the ad does not fit with the creative brief and it doesn't sell!

David Ogilvy initiated his own approach: the long-copy and tried to reconcile between the rational and the creative theories. He believed in the value of research and admitted that only a small percentage of consumers would read past the headline and the first paragraph of an ad, but he also realized that this small percentage happened to be those most interested in your product. And once you had the attention of this critical audience, you could tell them everything [49]. Interestingly, Ogilvy worshipped Claude Hopkins and provided a copy of *Scientific Advertising* to every employee, and he celebrated successful advertising from other agencies that tended to break all of his rules. Ogilvy did not like to say that he had or imposed rules, but nevertheless, here is advice from his book [31] that should be required reading for everybody working in advertising:

1. **Do your homework**- "Advertising people who ignore research are as dangerous as generals who ignore decoded enemy signals." [31] During the years he spent working for George Gallup, founder of the Gallup Poll, Ogilvy realized the true value that comes with knowing your target audience, what language they use when they discuss the subject, what attributes are important to them, and what promise would be more likely to make them buy your brand. He also recognized the importance of looking into what kind of advertising your competitors are engaging in.

2. **Positioning** "What the product does and who it is for." You cannot write copy unless you know: who you're writing it for, how that person thinks, and what that person needs.

3. **Brand image or personality** – What *image* you want for your brand. "The personality of a brand is an amalgam of its name, its

packaging, its price, the style of its advertising, and, above all, the nature of the product itself."

4. **What's the big idea** – "It takes a big idea to attract the attention of consumers and get them to buy your product." Ogilvy admitted he only had 20 big ideas (*unique, that fit the strategy to perfection, that works for 30 years*) in his life, and he used a process similar to Webb Young's to generate them.

5. **Make the product the hero** – "there are no dull products, only dull writers" – "explain your virtues more persuasively then your competitors, and differentiate them by the style of your advertising".

6. **The positively good** – it might not be necessary to convince consumers that your product is superior, and by doing so you might even insult their intelligence. It may be sufficient to convince them that your product is positively good: just say what's good about your product and do a clearer, more honest, more informative job than your competitors.

7. **Repeat your winners** – repeat your good advertisements until they stop selling.

8. **Don't get distracted from making the sale** "If it doesn't sell, it isn't creative."

In 1961, Russell Colley, a management consultant, claimed in his famous *Advertising Goals for Measured Advertising Results* [60] or **DAGMAR**, that is not possible to relate advertising to financial outcomes and proposed instead the theory of '**measurement by objectives**': brand awareness, advertising awareness, message recall, claimed usership, brand attitudes. He produces its own version of AIDA: Unawareness-Awareness-Comprehension-Conviction-Action.

The DAGMAR model asserts that advertising must be understood and believed before it can be acted upon, both questionable assumptions.

A Critique of the 'Creativity' theory

As senior executives know all too well, the desired end result of advertising should be financial (either sales or profits or both), and art and creativity are just a means of achieving this objective. Around 14% (or more) of creatively recognized campaigns failed to show any commercial success, usually because the strategy was wrong [10]. Unfortunately, those who regard advertising as a pure art form have a somewhat arrogant view, believe that if what they produce is creative or artistic, the consumer will magically adopt a favorable attitude towards the brand. In other words, *create it and they will come.* This is a somewhat naïve view of what it is like being a real artist: just look at the percentage of successful artists today. As shown in our Marketing Effectiveness model, creativity is just a part of it, although a very important one. Other more 'mundane' marketing elements need to come into play to make a brand successful: a good strategy, an adequate level of investment, distribution, marketing mix, and so on. At the end of the day, the best way to build most brands is with product-focused advertising. Usually, those who regard advertising as a pure art form are in a minority and they rarely have the final say in what advertisements are ultimately run [21].

Some creativity theories hugely undervalued the power of a strong claim or of detailed information. Martineau is wrong, in my view, when he claims that people cannot cope with words because they are brought up on an intellectual diet of Grade B movies and because the average human being is not a wordsmith, resulting in a deep distrust of advertisers that promote false or exaggerated assertions.

Instead, Reeves believed that "you can say four blunt words and a man will hit you in the face. You can tell a story and the same man will burst into tears" [46]. The truly valuable part of the brand-image theory is the power of the visual symbol, but the image of a brand is a subjective thing. No two people, however similar, hold precisely the same view of the same brands. Much of what influences the value of a brand lies in the hands of its competitors (because they too are building competing *mental structures* in the consumers' brain). The ambition to have a global brand (in the sense of consistent brand image worldwide) is therefore a contradiction in terms.

The non-rational aspects of choice are used today only in the sociological construct of *attitudes*, and any mention of *unconscious* is avoided for fear of ethical issues like manipulation of people's beliefs and behavior. The ways in which attitudes are understood and measured in research studies are dependent on verbal statements based on functional attributes (ex: brand X has a good taste) or projective techniques (ex: a brand for young people, a fashionable brand).

THE 'FAMILIARITY' OR 'FAME' THEORY

Marketers will spend a lot of time on finding the best copy strategy, arguing over adjectives in briefing documents, creating the best brand experience, or finding the best partnerships for the brand while ignoring the most probable avenue to business success: fame. Fame is based on a simple exposure theory, which suggests that consumers or customers form their preference based on familiarity triggered by mere exposure to the advertisement, rather than product/brand attribute information. Especially in low-involvement situations, when the simple fact that your brand is remembered may matter more than exactly what is remembered about the brand, recall alone is enough to lead to choice. The most extreme and controversial version of this **mere exposure effect** was developed by R.B. Zajonc in the 1960s. He hypothesized that preference is created by repeated exposure, at the preconscious level (i.e. without us being aware of it), with no associated cognitive activity. [35] According to this theory, salience or top-of-mind awareness, together with extensive distribution, are critically important. Advertising theoreticians A.S.C Ehrenberg and Gerald Tellis have emphasized that, for most mature brands, advertising works to reinforce (rather than create) brand preference, in the face of competitive advertisement, and that one way to do it is through high levels of reminder advertising, that use frequent repetition. [35] A related view (H.E. Krugman) is that repeated exposure creates a sense of familiarity with the brand, which creates positive feelings of *the pleasure of recognition*, comfort, security, ownership or intimacy, which in turn cause liking.

Fame works after all, even if its workings are complicated. I cannot say it better than Bob Hoffman: "You are massively more likely to be successful if you're famous. Fame is a monstrously huge advantage in business. If your brand is famous, retailers are far more likely to put you on their shelves, distributors are far more likely to pay attention to your calls, consumers are far more likely to buy your product, people are far more likely to serve your product to their guests, guys are far more likely to wear caps with your name on it, important people are far more likely to invite you to lunch, answer your emails, and meet you for a drink. And smart people are far more likely to want to work for you, be your lawyer, or sit on your board. But fame has a problem. It is not an elegant concept. It's too simple, crass, and obvious. It is not abstruse enough for most advertising and marketing executives. They get published and become 'experts' by creating arcane theories of consumer-brand relationships. They earn their stripes by taking the obvious and making it incomprehensible. They get their jobs by convincing CEOs and other erudite fakers that marketing is mysterious, and that understanding consumer behavior is a very complex and cryptic business. They think they know the mind of the consumer and how to manage it. And in doing so, they jump right over the most obvious and likely route to success." [22] Simply being famous, appearing to be ubiquitous and popular are no doubt important factors in brand building. In a recent example, beauty company Coty took a 51% stake in Kylie Cosmetics for $600 million, making Kylie Jenner, the 22-year-old founder of the makeup company and member of the Kardashian-Jenner family, the youngest billionaire in history. George Clooney and friend Rande Gerber sold Casamigos tequila, a brand they founded in 2013, to Diageo for $1 billion just four years later. In 2014, David Beckham and British entrepreneur Simon Fuller partnered with Diageo to release Haig Club, a single grain scotch whiskey. Beckham is said to have made millions from the partnership – one of the most lucrative of his career. [55] Diageo also partnered with P Diddy in 2007, bringing him on to help develop the Cîroc vodka brand. and then debuting another alcoholic beverage, DeLeón Tequila, in 2014.

Apart from celebrities' endorsements and collaborations, maximizing effective reach does not make anyone look particularly clever- neither the clients nor the agency...

Byron Sharp [56] demonstrated that:

- Brand size is almost entirely predictable based on brand penetration (more often than not, a brand can not grow if it does not recruit new buyers).
- People buy a repertoire of brands; brand loyalty is rare, and advertising works by reinforcing existing patterns of buying.

- Segmentation is in many ways a myth - different brands are bought by essentially the same kinds of people.
- Brands are not as different as business heads like to think. In fact, attitudes towards different brands are much more similar than they are different.

These findings led Ehrenberg and his colleagues in the 1980s to argue that the principal way advertising influences buying behavior is by making brands more salient, more accessible in more consumers' memory. Advertising is mere publicity: the role of creativity is neither to persuade nor to seduce, but merely to create images that are closely linked to the brand and which become lodged in the audience's long-term memory. Advertising does not create meaningful differentiation between brands, but meaningful distinctiveness. [56]

One practical implication of this theory is the following: most marketers nowadays working for international companies are just implementing campaigns that were created by a marketing team in the headquarters. They do not need to worry about the creativity of the campaign, if it is rational or emotional, they just need to adapt it to local specificities (most of the time meaning translation to the local language), create a media plan, and eventually put together several activation campaigns (events, sponsorships, promotions in key accounts and so on), with little autonomy in terms of changing the global concept and message. In this case, the only factor they have influence over is fame.

According to the fame theory, advertising success can all be boiled down to share of voice and brand salience. In 1975, King devised his *scale of immediacy*, in which different advertisements act in different ways, being either closer or further away from purchase, from the classic *buy now* inviting an immediate response to a brand image ad aiming to reinforce existing attitudes in order to defend brand share. [52] The fame theory is best exemplified, according to Batra, Myers and Aaker [4] by "studies suggesting that advertising repetition may in some situations itself lead to preference, even if consumers do not absorb information on product benefits. Such brand salience or top-of-mind awareness is especially important when the advertising is not so much at getting new consumers, but at reminding existing consumers to buy a particular brand." This is mostly the case for mature brands, when frequent repetition to create a continued sense of familiarity, safety, and comfort becomes one of the main advertising objectives. Especially in low-involvement situations, when consumers need to pick up a brand on their way out the door, memorable brands stand a much better chance of being selected, by entering the consideration phase without necessarily fulfilling the prerequisites for consideration.

Creating such familiarity, through awareness-building advertising (as well as extensive distribution and visibility at the point of sale) should be a more important advertising objective in situations when consumers are unlikely to extract much meaningful hard information from advertising [4]. Michael L. Ray and colleagues, in a series of studies done at Stanford University in the early 1970s, argued that when the products involved were of low involvement (low risk and low interest to the consumer), TV ads (nowadays this could apply to all video ads) did not lead to an information-based attitude change (like the rational persuasion theory would claim). Instead, the ads appeared to lead to purchase simply because of greater top-of-mind awareness, which ultimately resulted in a subconscious attitude change.

Robert Cialdini, the seminal expert in the field of influence and persuasion, confirms that for the most part, we like things that are familiar to us. Cialdini labels this phenomenon as *social proof,* a concept which maintains that we are reassured not just by our own familiarity with a brand name, but by the assumption that many others also use it [50]. Daniel Kahneman calls this behavior *availability heuristic*: things that we think of first or can picture most vividly are assumed to be most common and important. [50]

Both the rational persuasion and creativity theories conceptualize the advertising process as a one to one communication between the brand and individual consumer. However, the fame theory argues that the effects of advertising are largely social. Preference for the brand will be influenced by social context, by the perception that a brand is popular with others, a perception which advertising of sufficient ubiquity might create.

Les Binet and Peter Field conducted an excellent meta-analysis of hundreds of IPA Effectiveness cases. They classified campaigns by whether they are emotional, rational or focused on fame, ultimately concluding that the most powerful single force is, indeed, fame. Simply making a brand more famous drives sales.

Similarly, research by Amna Kirmani and Peter Wright have demonstrated that consumers use the perceived amount of advertising (*Share of Voice* or *Share of Experience*) as a proxy for brand quality and the advertiser's willingness to back that high quality with a high degree of marketing effort. Such a *signaling* effect though, works only as long as the consumer cannot find other justification for the high spending level (ex: the company desperate to move merchandise). [4]

The basic **share-of-voice model** provides a fairly accurate representation of how the average brand behaves. [6, 7] On average, brands that prioritize Share of Voice (SOV) above Share of Market (SOM) tend to gain market share, while brands that prioritize Share of Market above Share of Voice tend to experience a decline in market share.

There are some exceptions to this rule:

- **Big brands** (with a market share exceeding 20-30% in their category) tend to get away with a slightly lower SOV than one would expect from their SOM (most probably because of economies of scale not related to advertising: higher product quality and/or lower production costs, better commercial conditions with suppliers and customers, lower media buying costs, better commercial conditions with key accounts, a more loyal customer base, more PR coverage and word of mouth, etc.). Therefore, if a company has a large brand portfolio, a wise thing to do is to slightly underspend on advertising market leaders (especially if they are in flat or slightly declining categories) and overspend on smaller but promising brands (especially if they are in high growth categories).

This dichotomy between big and small brands is explained by the **double jeopardy** law, described by Romaniuk and Sharp from the Ehrenberg-Bass Institute [7]: smaller brands have fewer sales because they have fewer customers (the first jeopardy) who are also slightly less loyal (second jeopardy). This explains the market concentration that is occurring in almost all categories, as smaller brands are squeezed out. A consequence of the double jeopardy law is that focusing too much on loyalty, either by trying to build it or imagining it does not exist and thinking that you need to *buy* customers every time with price promotions or loyalty incentives, is a costly distraction that brands can often not afford. On the other hand, it is easy for managers of big brands to become complacent by highlighting consistently high metrics (some of them just vanity metrics, like number of ad views) and allow smaller competitors to slowly erode their market share. This an opportunity for small brands that we will address in Chapter 8.

- **New and niche brands** (less than 1-2% share) with low budgets. We will explain this case below, in the Social Connection Theory section.

Another problem with this theory is related to the difficulty of calculating Share of Voice: digital expenditures are well known for your brand but can only be estimated for competitor brands, as Google and Facebook are very opaque and do not provide this information, while traditional media SOV is also difficult to calculate (but not impossible).

Critique of Fame Theory

The DAGMAR project and research by David W. Stewart and colleagues have established that recall of the ad (awareness) is necessary for comprehension of the ad content, and comprehension of the ad content is necessary for persuasion, but such persuasion also requires message content that sets the brand apart as being superior to its competition. At least in high-involvement situations, the ad must not only create awareness and recall, it must also include content to which consumers react favorably, by generating favorable cognitive responses.

Another reason why recall may be unrelated to persuasion may simply be that whatever does get recalled about a brand at the time the consumer is about to choose is successful in getting the brand to the consideration phase but simply not enough to influence the actual brand selection decision. [35] Therefore, advertisers have two major objectives: to place into the consumers' memory the brand-differentiating features that the consumer is likely to use in making a choice and that prove the brand is superior, and to ensure these attributes must be easily accessible in the consumer memory. Fame Theory addresses only the second part of this equation.

THE SOCIAL CONNECTION THEORY

Social connection is an interesting phenomenon, as exemplified in the recent success of artisanal (or craft) brands. They can get away with a low share of voice because, as the Bass diffusion model (first outlined by Franck Bass in 1969) predicts, for any innovation, there is a pool of potential adopters. Some will adopt it on their own, without any advertising or very limited advertising (the *innovators* and *the early adopters*), while the others are imitators (*early majority, late majority* and *laggards*). In the early phase, growth is exponential due to innovators and early adopters, who tell their friends about the new, hot thing on the market. During this time, advertising might seem unnecessary, word-of-mouth alone will do the trick.

Many alcohol brands, including craft brands, were built through personal contact with consumers, prescriptors, or *advocates*, like bartenders, bar owners, and brand ambassadors, communities, or just regular consumers. As Paul Ricard, the inventor of Ricard pastis (a famous alcoholic drink from Marseille, with a strong aniseed taste, launched in 1975 which became the No1 selling spirit brand in France) used to say to his sales teams: *make a friend every day* and *the consumer is our best sales rep*. Paul Ricard thought of communication as a kind of *collective celebration*. His analysis was simple: there is no life in society without parties. And there are no parties without alcohol (for those over the legal drinking age, of course). Over the years, Ricard undertook the unofficial title of the king of French parties and celebrations, participating in countless concerts, tournaments, festivals, and so forth, truly staying true to his aforementioned advertising dogma.

In fact, product experience dominates advertising for goods for which product quality can be judged through inspection and low-experience goods for which little experience is required before quality can be assessed. [41]

This explains why, for example, many beverage brands spend a substantial percentage of their advertising budgets on brand events, like concerts, music festivals, or live events. A lot of people with a data-driven approach to advertising underestimate the power of live engagement and believe that as long as they can get to people as often as they can (usually through digital advertisement) they will win, not realizing that frequency of contact can be also annoying and counterproductive (see Chapter 4, Effective frequency), unless you build an emotional connection. For example, music creates a mood and emotional response, which explains why events and entertainment in general are so powerful in building brands and creating mental availability. When people are in a mood for being entertained, as they are when they go to a music festival, for example, they are less open to information through traditional mediums such as print. In fact, an old advertising saying is: *when you have nothing to say, sing it!* Advertising is a critical part of popular culture, with all that it includes, like drama, humor, music, rituals, games, sex appeal, dance, costumes, and sport.

The power of public events is in creating word of mouth through communities of people that share the same passions. Many brands have understood the importance of helping, supporting, and participating in clubs, associations and communities built on the sharing of passion: petanque and rugby (Ricard), dogs (Tito's vodka), extreme sports (Red Bull), barbecue and Harley-Davidson motor clubs (Jack Daniel's), art lovers (Absolut), and so on. By starting a relationship with the leaders of these communities, the brands came to play a role in their everyday life and became a cult brand. Red Bull, which created a community around extreme sports, sees itself as a producer of content rather than an advertiser. These are just a few examples of how successful it can be to influence the public through the power of story and sense of community, by creating relationships, and above all through the visual image and association with passion points.

Human communication is extremely important in creating a relationship with your brand, even in today's technological society. The advertiser often needs to provide information, to have a trustworthy and consistent message, to be repetitive, to sell hard, as well as to charm and to entertain. Social scientists have discovered a number of factors that reliably cause liking, which in turn drives sales: the physical attractiveness of the salespersons or promoters (see the Jägerettes example), similarity (we like people that are similar to us), compliments (like the postcards that 'the greatest car salesman' Joe Girard sent every month to his potential customers, with only a few words printed on them: *I like you*), and finally contact and cooperation (the principle behind brand ambassadors).

Advertising is not only about content, be it rational or seductive, it is also about relationships: between the consumer and the brand, between the sales staff and the customers. It is about customer interactions either in real life or on social media. It is also about execution: the quality and attention to detail of the implementation of a brilliant campaign in retail or on-premise. It is about the tone of voice, the connotative use of language, all factors that conventional advertising theories treat as afterthoughts.

Critique of Social Connection Theory

As Mark Ritson argues in his column hosted by Marketing Week, in his message to Elon Musk regarding the need for Tesla to advertise, the traditional models of brand-building (rational persuasion, fame, or creativity) do not need to be followed to achieve commercial success in the early stages of a brand. But after a certain level of sales and profitability have been reached, thanks to organic media (from PR) and influencers, there are many advantages to be had from even a modest investment in ad spend. By committing to large-scale, big-brand advertising you send a clear message to everyone that your brand is not a fad or uncertain business, but one of the successful brands which can afford to pay top dollar for media to further increase awareness and reach 'the silent, boring majority who do not really follow what is actually going on, but can be reached through advertising'. [43] Sooner or later, your newsworthiness is going to wane and the loyalty of influencers that helped your brand to take off will decline as they move to the next new thing, so advertising will become essential in order to sustain growth, retain, and defend your market share dominance. Furthermore, in order to reduce price sensitivity, in the face of new entrants and increased competition, you need to have a strong brand, and this can be achieved largely through traditional advertising models.

 CONCLUSIONS

Advertising is not just one thing: there are many types of advertising and they serve many different purposes for many strategic objectives and many different types of business. In this challenging environment, knowing the different theories of advertising and how they apply to different situations is paramount to successfully influencing consumers' attitudes. Winning brands will be the ones that best interpret this new reality, all while remaining consistent with their positioning, inner DNA, and individual story.

Looking at the past is important for understanding the underlying principles that made the old campaigns work because these underlying principles are still valid. The history of how advertising works has been led by the changes in the dominant media channels: from face-to-face salesmanship to direct mail and print, to TV, and now to digital. But the principles behind how advertising theories exist independently of media channels and depending on your advertising objective and available budget may still be applicable today (see example below in Table 1).

The millennial generation has grown up learning how to avoid advertising across all forms of media, therefore the only ads that are going to survive are those that delight. These ads must achieve a balance between familiarity and novelty. There are aspects of advertising that are scientific, based on neuroscience or the work of the Ehrenberg Bass Institute. However, at the same time, brand-building advertising is a craft, it is artistry, and execution is very important. To paraphrase Paul Feldwick: consumers do not buy musical notes, they buy the actual music.

I do not believe that there is a dichotomy in advertising between rational persuasion vs emotional influence, science vs art, creativity vs technology, intuition vs data. They can and should work together if you want to achieve marketing excellence, as explained in the Marketing Phronesis concept.

To quote Rory Sutherland: "In his book Skin in the Game (2018), Taleb includes what might be the most interesting quotation on an individual's politics I have ever read. Someone explains how, depending on the context, he has entirely different political preferences: At the federal level I am a Libertarian. At the state level, I am a Republican. At the town level, I am a Democrat. In my family, I am a socialist. And with my dog, I am a Marxist – from each according to his abilities, to each according to his needs." [27]

Another great figure in advertising, David Ogilvy, tried to argue both for the power of brand image and the importance of creativity, and for the centrality of rational persuasion and the value of research-based rules, and I personally feel drawn to his ideas. The current status of how advertising works is that both Rational and Creativity models are accepted as *Traditional Advertising Models*. The rational theory because it allows advertising to be planned and researched on the basis that an advertisement must first attract attention, then transmit a message or proposition, which has to be understood, believed, and remembered. The creativity theory because artistry has been and continues to be an essential ingredient in attracting attention, increasing the memorability of the message, and establishing a preference for a particular brand based on emotional and non-verbal cues. Challenges to this dual model and balance of powers have an impact on power relations within the advertising company and between the company and its ad agency.

Here is my summary of how different theories work out best:

Table 1: How advertising theories work

	Rational persuasion	Creativity	Fame	Social connection
Principle	Salesmanship/ Reason Why	Create likable feeling	Share of Voice>Share of Market	Focus on early adopters
Works best in:	D2C/ eCommerce/B2B	Prestige brands	Mature brands	Small/craft brands
	Innovation using rational message	Credence products	When no brand is clearly dominant	Small budgets
	Training salesforce	Low involvement situations	Big budgets	Low involvement categories
	High involvement categories	Peripheral cues, executional elements	Low experience	High experience
	Search products	Using attractive or credible spokespersons	Low involvement situations-no cognitive activity	
	Consumers' high motivation and ability to process information	Consumers' motivation or ability are low		

Legend:

High experience – considerable use required before quality can be assessed (ex: cars)

Low experience – little use required before quality can be assessed (ex: alcohol)

Credence – quality can not be determined even after experience (ex: fashion)

Search – product quality can be judged through inspection

Table 2: Channel choice based on objectives - example

	Awareness	Consideration	Trial	Usage
Audience	Core	Core	Broad	Broad
Channel that best suits objective	TV, OOH	Digital, Displays	Packaging, POS, Sampling	Experiential

Figure 5: A lifecycle advertising model for a low involvement category brand

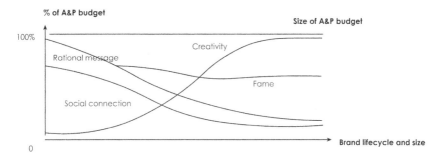

The dilemmas we are struggling with today are not new, and because buyer behavior is so complicated, a general theory is not achievable. Our understanding of how advertising works can only be furthered by studying where our predecessors have already been.

What is the solution then? My theory is that we must combine both theory and practice, while considering the context in which the practice occurred, to build a comprehensive Phronesis marketing concept. More about this in Chapter 5.

A WORD ABOUT MARKETING PREDICTIONS

Is it possible to make predictions in marketing in general? Probably not.

American Way Magazine calls marketing guru Seth Godin *America's Greatest Marketer*, his blog being the most popular marketing blog in the world. However, in 1996, Seth Godin predicted that by the year 2000, internet banner ads would be gone. If even the greatest in the industry can be wrong, what hope is there for the mere mortals?

In 1983, David Ogilvy, founder of Ogilvy & Mather, and known as the *Father of Advertising*, made the following predictions about the future of marketing in his famous book, *Ogilvy on Advertising* [31]:

1. The quality of research will improve, and this will generate a bigger corpus of knowledge as to what works and what doesn't. Creative people will learn to exploit this knowledge, thereby improving their strike rate at the cash register.
2. There will be a renaissance in print advertising.
3. Advertising will contain more information and less hot air.
4. Billboards will be abolished.
5. The clutter of commercials on television and radio will be brought under control.
6. There will be a vast increase in the use of advertising by governments for purposes of education, particularly health education.
7. Advertising will play a part in bringing the population explosion under control.
8. Candidates for political office will stop using dishonest advertising.

9. The quality and efficiency of advertising overseas will continue to improve –at an accelerating rate. More foreign tortoises will overtake the American hare.

10. Several foreign agencies will open offices in the United States and will prosper.

11. Multinational manufacturers will increase their market shares all over the non-Communist world, and will market more of their brands internationally. The advertising campaigns for these brands will emanate from the headquarters of multinational agencies but will be adapted to respect differences in the local culture.

12. Direct-response advertising will cease to be a separate specialty and will be folded into the 'general' agencies.

13. Ways will be found to produce effective television commercials at a more sensible cost.

I argue that more than half of his predictions were not accurate. This is not to reduce the merits of Ogilvy, who is a giant in advertising history, but to show how difficult it is to predict how advertising will evolve, the main reason being the impossibility to predict the technological advances and societal changes that will impact the way that consumers interact with brands.

So why do we talk so much about the future? Because the present is a dangerous place to be, and it's boring. The future is much sexier.

TWO

Can marketing be made accountable by measuring ROI?

It is not uncommon for marketing managers to be criticized by their peers, usually commercial or finance managers, for a lack of accountability to commercial realities. It is true that marketers tend to get carried away by the artistic side of marketing and forget they need to also sell.

There is an increasing emphasis in modern marketing on justifying expenditures to the nearest dollar in order to calculate ROI. While this focus on accountability is good, there is a risk of going to the other extreme and using ROI inappropriately in a way that diminishes the value of good marketing.

So what is ROI? It is a financial indicator that can be used to measure the return for any type of investment. The formula is simple: it is the revenue generated by your marketing efforts divided by the expenditure.

Let's consider a simple ROI calculation, starting with a baseline, or the margin made in a regular month with the company's regular marketing efforts, be those endorsements or event marketing. Let's suppose the company regularly makes a $100,000 profit margin on a $10,000 investment in any given month. Now let's suppose that this company decides to increase its marketing budget by $15,000 in one month to conduct a direct marketing campaign which costs $25,000$ and results in a $120,000 margin. Then the gross contribution of that campaign is (120,000-100,000)=$20,000, and the net contribution is 20,000-15,000=$5,000. In this case the ROI is 5,000/15,000= 33% return (of $1.33 return for every $1 'invested').

This looks like a great achievement, but there are several issues with this calculation:

- Marketing expenditure is only a part of the company's total cost to deliver that sale. For example, if a company has very high SGA (salaries, rent, utilities and other administrative costs), a return of 33% might not cover your costs; or the value generated (in this case, $20,000 in additional margin) is too small to cover costs
- Marketing expenditure is not the only reason that extra margin is generated: you could have a new listing during the month, or a sales promotion, or the competition may have been delisted from an account. This is called **the attribution problem.**

- The baseline calculation might be difficult to calculate due to different factors, including seasonality, distribution changes, etc.
- Focusing on monthly or quarterly ROI as the source of truth tends to encourage short term activities and retention, i.e. targeting existing or loyal customers. When you do that you are likely generating sales that would have occurred anyway. The danger is that, by ignoring recruitment (non-users of the brand), you are preventing brand growth and a loss of market share will occur sooner or later.
- The easiest way to increase ROI is to reduce marketing spend. If you cut marketing spent to almost zero, ROI will go through the roof! But this will result in reduced sales and market share over time.
- Those focusing on ROI do not usually mean an investment in one year that delivers sales and profits in future years, but expenditure that results in revenue in the same year. But advertising ROI makes more sense when it is truly an investment, in other words when payback comes in later years. In which case, the present value of the investment (i.e. discounted cash flow minus the cost of the investment) or payback (how long will it take to recover the cost of the investment) is a better alternative to ROI [33] . But it usually takes a long period of time (more than two years, most probably five years) to calculate DCF, and managers often cannot wait this long to evaluate their marketing investment. I will describe an alternative method in detail in Chapter 4.
- And last but not least, the idea that the objective of marketing has changed from creating value to the consumer to creating shareholder value goes too far, although this simplification is useful to remind the marketer about shareholders' expectations. [33]

Therefore, ROI must be used carefully and applied over longer periods of time. Focus on the short-term ROI of a marketing investment has in large part led to a rise in digital advertising and a general decrease in advertising creativity.

Marketing ROI is not linear, but rather 'S' shaped: below a certain level, marketing investments do not lead to sales, and beyond a certain threshold incremental marketing investments start providing returns. That is why optimization efforts based purely on plug-and-play ROI calculations might wrongly recommend a reduction of marketing budgets while the brand is in the initial phase. Beyond an upper limit, however, additional investments do not lead to a corresponding increase in sales (i.e. the law of diminishing returns).

Figure 6:The 'S' curve

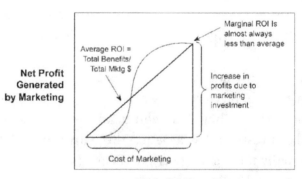

THREE
The science and art of building a company strategy

As an advertiser, one of the frequent questions asked by advertising agencies and consultants is: how do you build your strategic plan and your budget? In Figure 7, I attempt to summarize the annual budget process, from a brand perspective, for a multi-country, multi-brand company.

Figure 7: Annual budgeting process

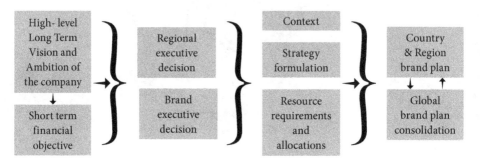

In smaller companies, the executive management (usually just a few people, most probably the founders) have an implicit strategy as opposed to a formal strategy process. However, the company generally feels the need to review the company strategy on a regular basis and reflect on where it stands and what direction to take.

In bigger and more complex companies, there is a formalized strategic process, because the different departments and business units need to be aligned and the number of people involved in the strategic process is quite important. A strategic planner generally leads the strategy process, with a relatively small team of professionals, situated at the headquarters, most often in conjunction with the finance department. A formal strategy process is carried out at fixed times every year, with meetings set up between relevant stakeholders. Senior management usually sets the overall direction, strategic pillars, and targets for its divisions or business units, and the business units commit to accomplishing a portion of the targets by first taking into consideration the environment and competitive context. This series of meetings result in strategy documents and presentations, which are sent up to the management board for approval so that the execution can begin.

The budget process is often a political struggle: the business manager tends to present a bright future for the unit he is responsible for, with the caveat that the next few years will likely present challenges, both financial and executional. The reason for this approach is simple: you want top management to see you are aggressive in the medium and long term, proving that you are a great manager, but you also want to get out of the budget meeting with an attainable budget objective so that you and your team can achieve your desired bonus.

To avoid this conflict of interest, the company should strive for an efficient and effective budget process, as portrayed in Figure 8 below.

Figure 8: Optimizing Strategic Planning Process

In order to avoid the effectiveness-efficiency dilemma, I think that the dual approach: top-down and bottom-up is best to achieve ambitious, but reasonable targets that motivate the team without leaving money on the table.

Effective marketing starts with a clear strategy: you need to make sure you have long-term corporate objectives (a *strategic plan*) which will drive annual marketing strategy (*annual budgets*) and short-term marketing programs and operations (quarterly *drive cycles* and monthly *implementations plans*).

Figure 9: Marketing Strategic Plan

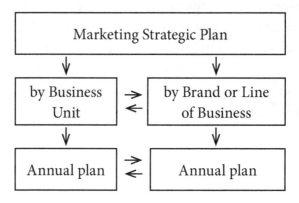

Your strategic plan has to identify and prioritize the key inflection points that can accelerate your topline and bottom-line growth.

Marketing leaders can use this guide to create robust strategic marketing plans that deliver SMART objectives (Specific, Measurable, Assignable, Relevant, and Time-Bound).

STEP 1: LONG-TERM VISION AND AMBITION

WHAT Articulate your vision and ambition for the company and for the brands and business units, and identify any possible Inflection points that will help you achieve them

OUTPUT

Market segmentation

Market segmentation is central not only to marketing but to every strategic corporate function.

It is necessary to understand and define the markets the organization operates in, for example:

o From general category to specific : Does your brand fall within the spirits & wine business, the spirits business, the premium spirits business, the international premium spirits business, or only the prestige international premium spirits business ?

o Product only or product and services/new business : Do your brands fall within the spirits business or spirits & services/new business associated with spirits drinking?

Once market(s) have been defined, it is necessary to understand their value, both financially and in terms of customer value requirements.

– Market prioritization and resource allocation, by market and brand (see example below)
– Category growth opportunities that provide a possibility for accelerated growth (see example below)
– Geographic expansion, innovation or new business opportunities
– Initiatives related to brand equity (ex: rejuvenations, brand extensions, and brand repositioning)
– Pricing strategies and premiumization

ESSENTIALS

All of the above have to be supported by a clear rationale, have to be quantified and prioritized, and have to include investments needed to get there, as well as KPIs and deadlines.

Figure 10: Market prioritization and
resource allocation by market

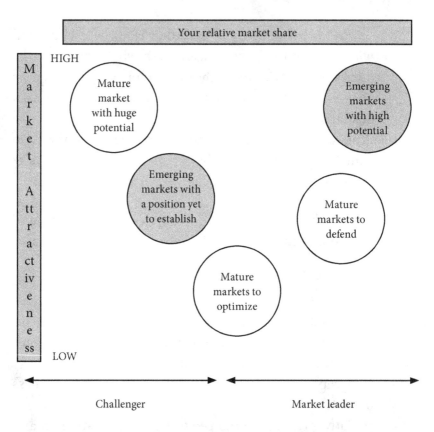

Market attractiveness is a combination of market size, growth rate, incremental middle-class households, profitability, and consumption per capita.

Figure 11: Market prioritization and resource allocation by brand

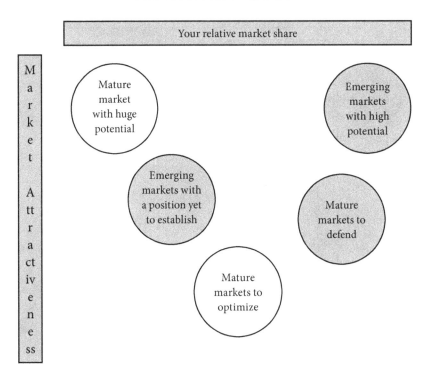

Category attractiveness is a combination of category size, profitability, category forecast and barriers to entry.

Figure 12: Category growth opportunity

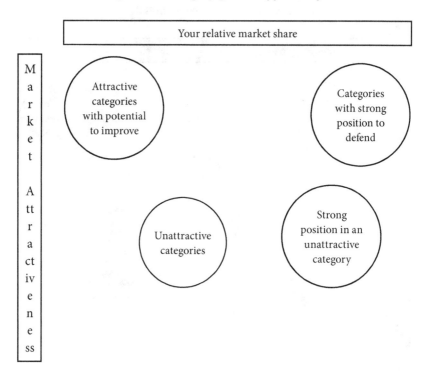

Note: Relative share corresponds to your company relative share vs market leader or #2 when you are the leader

 STEP 2: CONTEXT

WHAT General industry/market/brand context

OUTPUT

- *Explaining the Past*: Financial performance and market shares by region, market, category, and brands and how these have evolved over time, as well as *key learnings from the past* – which objectives were achieved, which were not, and why.

- *Prepare for the future*: Key macroeconomic indicators, such as geopolitics and regulations, competition, trade, and macro consumer trends.

ESSENTIALS

Objective assessments are based both on internal and external sources. Key inputs and techniques include marketing and financial analysis, SWOT, and other consultant-type analysis.

Figure 13: Comparative performance between brands in the past

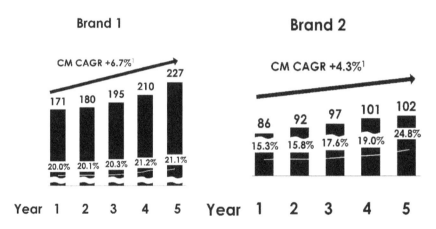

STEP 3: STRATEGY FORMULATION

WHAT Key drivers for the plan, by region, market, and brand

OUTPUT Presents in detail how you will get from the current status quo to the desired one:

- Route to Market

- Route to Consumer
- De-prioritizations
- Human Resources and organizational changes

ESSENTIALS

Marketing objectives and strategies are accompanied by goal setting, key success factors, and KPIs. Targets and metrics should use the SMART format.

Table 3: Marketing objectives key success factors and KPIs

Brand inflection points	Relevant channel(s)	Expected Growth %	Expected Growth $	Status
Key Objective 1				
Key Objective 2…				

STEP 4: RESOURCE REQUIREMENTS AND ALLOCATIONS

When running a global or international business, the issue of resource allocation is probably the most difficult. How much money should we allocate in region X vs region Y? What brand should receive an increased investment and which brand should we de-prioritize?

WHAT Resource allocation rationale by market, brand, and key business drivers

OUTPUT

Budgets and resource plans (marketing, operations, technology, people, training etc.) supporting the delivery of the strategy described in Step 3. This should reflect the capability of the company to invest, as well as the current organizational maturity to support the strategy.

ESSENTIALS

Allocations informed by the short-term, mid-term, and long-term projected benefits that strategies will deliver to the business and by a review of current-state and desired marketing maturity.

Table 4: Resource allocation by key business driver

Key Business Driver	1yr impact ($)	3yr impact	5yr impact	Current state	Marketing maturity status
KBD1					
.....					

Solid marketing strategies set a clear direction for one to three years but should be able to be understood by the whole organization and not only by top management. The changing nature of the environment, which is increasingly volatile in recent years, has made long-term planning cycles increasingly difficult to achieve.

Consider the following factors that can have an influence on your marketing strategy:

External factors

External factors that are outside the control of the organization (ex: economic changes – exchange rates, interest rates, duties and taxes, laws and regulations), social and cultural changes (ex: the rise in more eco-friendly, sustainable products), or technological shifts (ex: *uberisation* of the industry).

However, there are also external factors that are at least somewhat within the control of the organization (ex: changes in competition set and offer, shifts in customer behavior (ex: buying fewer products in general but more premium products), or changes in the distribution channel (ex: increase of discounters and private labels, e-commerce).

Table 5: Examples of key consumer trends driving product innovation and their expression

New take on something familiar	Real stories	Social status reinforcement	Healthy hedonism	Doing good for the planet	Doing good for the society
-New Flavors	-Craft -Real people behind brands -Retro	-Premiumization -Indulgence	-Organic -Low sugar -Super plants	-Recyclable packaging -Responsible sourcing -CO2 neutral	-Charity link

Internal factors

Factors inside the organization can impact as well the performance (ex: first-semester performance requires cut in marketing budget to protect profitability, new investor joins the business and wants a further increase in profitability, a new business opportunity requires extra investment and resource reallocation, key talent leaves the business, etc.).

CRITIQUE OF LONG-TERM PLANNING

A major problem with long-term planning is tunnel vision. All the systems discussed in this chapter rely on projecting the present into the future. If nothing much changes - neither the environment, the competitors, nor consumer preferences, then indeed the future will look much like the present, but as we can see lately, this has become very unlikely. The world has become more unpredictable, and events that seemed improbable just a few years ago occur today without much shock from the general public. Under these circumstances, planning for the long-term has become almost impossible. On top of this, planning during uncertain times can become a very time consuming exercise that takes away resources perhaps better used in business development.

Nevertheless, based on my experience, it is a useful exercise that should be done every 3 years in tandem with the annual budget creation, focusing on essentials.

 ## BUDGET/PLAN IMPROVEMENTS

During the budgeting process, make sure brand plans include:

- clear business effectiveness objectives and the corresponding metrics and follow-up necessary to determine how well the investment met its objectives
- rigorously track metrics over time (business and brand reviews)
- employ a classic account planning process (*disciplined creativity*)
- rely on a rigorous methodology for budget allocations by country, brand, and category

FOUR

How to build a successful marketing strategy

 ## 4.1 HOW DO COMPANIES SET UP THEIR MARKETING BUDGETS?

For many companies, budgeting time is in the autumn. It is that time of the year when marketing managers and their CEOs and CFOs sit to discuss next year's revenues and margin forecast and how much they will spend on marketing activities. Setting budgets is always an iterative process, always including much back and forth between different stakeholders until the numbers look right for all the parties. You will find that your preparation and involvement in this process as a marketing executive will be one of the main factors contributing to the success or failure of your activities, second only perhaps to the execution itself.

Consumer goods companies tend to differ from B2B companies in their budgeting approach, so let's have a look at the five different types of budgeting:

1. Whatever You Can Afford
2. % of Forecasted Sales
3. Competitive Benchmark
4. Objective and Task
5. Modeling

1. The *Whatever You Can Afford* method

Many marketers set their budgets based on what they can afford (especially if they have known cash limitations) in order to increase the probability that it will be approved by their management. This is by far the safest and easiest way to get your budget approved, but not the recommended method, as the chances to deliver the best business results are significantly lower. Nevertheless, it is still used by many B2C and B2B companies, particularly start-ups.

2. The *Percentage of Forecasted Sales* method

This method is likely the most common approach to budgeting for CPG companies: it takes into consideration the forecasted sales for next year (net of eventual taxes) and chooses a reasonable % for the marketing budget. The percentage can be higher than last year if the management thinks they were under-investing, if they want to gain market share, or if the market is a priority market. Some companies have adopted the P&A (Profit and Advertising) approach, which assumes that margins are directly proportional with advertising and therefore advertising budget is calculated as a % of forecasted margins to achieve at least a zero marginal contribution to bottom line.

The *percentage of sales* method assumes that marketing expenditure is a result of sales, while in reality, it is exactly the opposite! Nevertheless, it is the most common way of budgeting due to its simplicity and acceptance within the vast majority of organizations.

A variation of this is applied for a brand portfolio: some brands within the portfolio, which are in categories of higher growth or are in the seed/launch phase get higher % of the budget, while brands in a lower growth category get a lower % of sales in advertising.

This method is not commonly used by B2B companies, with a few exceptions.

3. The *Competitive Benchmarking* method

This method assumes that competitors' marketing expenditures represent the so-called *collective wisdom* of the industry. In other words, the industry knows better what is good and will adjust collective expenditures accordingly based on the socio-economic context. One common approach is to compare Share of Voice (SOV) with Share of Market (SOM). If SOV>=SOM, the company is in a good position and has higher chances to gain market share; if not, it might consider increasing its marketing expenditure to catch up with the competition. There are of course exceptions to this rule, for example if a company has a dominant position.

Since listed companies have to publish their P&Ls, the percentage of marketing vs sales expenditure is, of course, public information. A company using this method is constantly checking their main competitors' ratios and adjusting their budget upwards or downwards, depending on how they compare to the other players. The method is often used by consultants and financial investors and analysts to compare companies within the same industry. A company that achieves a better performance with a lower %

of advertising/sales expenditure is usually considered better at utilizing its resources, although over time this under-investment might result in a loss of market share.

The disadvantages of this method:

-   Benchmarking might not be possible if your main competitors are not listed and therefore this information is more difficult if not impossible to obtain, or if your competitors are listed but do not publish specific data for your market in order to benchmark against your own.
-   Share of voice is easy to calculate for traditional media, but not easy for digital and can even be impossible for non-media (ex: events).
-   It is sometimes difficult to calculate your share of voice if your category is not easy to define or there is more than one way to define it.
-   Advertising expenses might be difficult to calculate due to lack of transparency across channels.
-   The method does not take into consideration the quality of the content.
-   And finally, what if your competitors are all wrong, meaning they are all under-investing or over-investing?

4. The *Objective-and-Task* method

A more sophisticated approach is the *objective-and-task* method. The marketer starts by defining his or her marketing objectives, by brand, based on the performance of the brand and its strategic assessment. The next step is to determine the tasks that must be performed in order to achieve this objective (ex: in order to increase spontaneous awareness within the housewives segment from 15% to 17% by the end of the next calendar year, I need to do *informative* vs *persuasive* vs *reminder* advertising, etc.), which in turn informs the advertising development. The marketer then creates a cost estimate based on those tasks, along with a project timeline.

In practice, one way of doing this is through the auction technique: the first draft marketing plan with quantified objectives is agreed upon by the local team with the brand owner (in terms of campaigns and KPIs) and then shared with the partner agencies (could be different agencies for media, experiential marketing, and PR, depending on the size of the budget and the quality of the agencies in the local market). Then the agencies bid for the resources they could best use towards those objectives and the results that can be expected.

Another way to do it is to use last year's plan and run a simulation (explained in Chapter 3), based on objectives, actual touchpoint cost, restrictions in terms of minimum thresholds by touchpoint, and maximizing the Effective Reach with the same amount of money.

How to choose objectives is based on the process described in Chapter 3 and 4.

The disadvantage of this method is that it does not indicate whether the cost of attaining these objectives are worthwhile.

5. Modelling methods

Different types of decision support systems have been developed recently, not only in regard to the size of the marketing budget but also its allocation by touchpoint. In essence, the models look to maximize *net margin* minus *advertising expenses*, either by using response models (S-curve) or econometrics.

The S-shaped response model is generally well accepted within many industries, although Broadbent (1984) has proven that data uncertainty and methodological questions make either proving or disproving the S-shaped hypothesis problematic. The main assumption behind the S-shape response are:

- Diminishing returns on advertising spend (magnitude of the sales increase will decrease over time)
- Sales decay takes place more slowly than sales growth (the rise is related to advertising spent, the decline is related to product experience and competition)

In practice, many modern modeling methodologies (including SaaS) use the *Objective and Task* method in conjunction with either econometrics or modeling/algorithms.

Advances in the availability of data and in measurement, particularly POS or e-commerce data, are refining our understanding of how advertising works and my prediction is that, in the near future, the modelling methods combined with *Objective and Task* methods will gain traction because they deliver better advertising decisions than their alternatives.

Some advice for companies operating in multiple geographies:

- Use the same methodology across markets to be able to compare results
- Create a database with all relevant tests done, in order to allow for benchmarking
- Create a cost database with touchpoints by country, in order to compare results

4.2 IS ORDER OF MARKET ENTRY A COMPETITIVE ADVANTAGE?

Many empirical research studies have investigated the existence of a competitive advantage associated with being the first to enter a category. The belief (endorsed by studies like PIMS) is that the brands that invent a (sub)category experience a stronger business performance in terms of market share. We wanted to test the conclusions of the PIMS study for the spirit industry to find out if this is true, or partially true (i.e. only for some categories).

In the late 1970s, industry studies documented long-lived market share advantages for first entrants in pharmaceutical products (Bond and Lean, 1977) and cigarettes (Whitten, 1979). On the other hand, in other categories, pioneers were quickly overtaken by later entrants, like in the diet cola industry. Royal Crown Cola, now owned by Keurig Dr. Pepper, introduced the first diet cola, Diet Rite, to the public in 1958 but was soon overtaken by its bigger, more famous rivals.

In the 80s two papers, using PIMS data (the Profit Data of Marketing Strategy Project of research in marketing strategy) suggested that market pioneers tend to have higher-than-average market shares, relative to later entrants and that the share advantages tend to last for decades.

Table 6: Order of entry and market share in Consumer goods

	Concentrated markets	Fragmented markets
Market pioneers	34%	12%
Early followers	24%	7%
Later entrants	17%	6%

Source: Parry and Bass (1990)

It seems the main reason why market pioneers tend to have higher market shares compared to later entrants is that they have higher perceived product quality, although this higher perceived product quality advantage tends to disappear after 20 years. Another reason would be that risk-averse consumers tend to buy the pioneering brand out of habit, and that first experiences help shape consumer tastes in favor of the pioneering brand.

Table 7: Order of entry and ROI, by business maturity (consumer goods)

	Start-up (yrs. 1 - 4)	Adolescent (yrs. 5 - 8)	Mature
Market pioneers	-23%	21%	25%
Early followers	-17%	18%	19%
Later entrants	-17%	9%	16%

Source: Parry and Bass (1990)

According to Table 7, it seems that, while a market pioneering strategy is both costly and risky, successful pioneers also enjoy higher ROI than early followers and later entrants.

Now let's see if this is true for spirits brands. In Table 8, we looked at a few famous successful innovations in the spirits industry:

Table 8: Spirits inventions and innovations

(Sub)Category	"Inventor"/Launch year	Market leader 2018/ Launch year
Whisky based honey liqueur	Wild Turkey Honey/2007	Jack Daniels Tennessee Honey/2011
Premium vodka	Absolut/1979	Absolut
Super Premium vodka	Belvedere/1996	Grey Goose/1997
Super Premium gin	Hendricks/1999	Hendricks
Pink Gin	Puerto de Indias/2013	Gordon's Pink gin/2017
Cinnamon-flavored whisky	Fireball/1985	Jack Daniels Tennessee Fire/2015

The most obvious key success factors are the bottle (an old Victorian apothecary's bottle for Hendricks, vintage Swedish apothecary bottle for Absolut, or a see-through frozen elongated bottle for Grey Goose), the country of origin and what it is famous for (Grey Goose vodka is made in the Cognac region, Absolut vodka is made in Sweden of pure water). Based on the table above, you can see that the rule of first market entry does not always apply to the spirits industry. Instead, being a big brand or being bought and/ or distributed by a big company can make a huge difference. Jack Daniels flavors became leaders due to the strength of its mother brand, despite being second in the market, 20 years behind the innovators, while brands like Puerto de Indias (currently HIG Capital) or Fireball (Sazerac), owned by investment funds or smaller companies, will probably never get back to No. 1, although they invented the category, because their bigger competitors outplayed them. According to Erwin Maldonado, Global Chief Marketing Officer at Puerto de Indias, despite inventing the strawberry/ pink gin category in 2013 and the fact that it is still the leader in Spain, with over 55% market share, the global leader in pink gin is Gordon's due to its market share in the UK (90% market share in a market that is double the size of Spain's) and also the global distribution power of Diageo, Gordon's owner.

4.3 THE FOUR KEY PILLARS OF A SUCCESSFUL MARKETING STRATEGY

It is universally accepted that brands are a company's most valuable asset, yet there is no universally accepted method of measuring that value. Unfortunately, the only time you can be sure of the value of your brand is just after you've sold it.

Figure 14: The four pillars of a successful marketing strategy

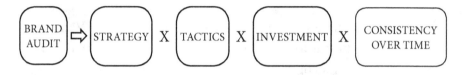

4.3.1 Brand Audit

The objective of a Brand Audit is to do a brand health check in order to understand performance and drivers.

To understand what can go wrong with a brand, we need to look at why brands fail. There are several reasons for brand identity failures [29]:

- **Brand ego** or brand arrogance: brands can overestimate their importance to their consumers and either spend below maintenance level, or not pay enough attention to customer service or the quality of their brand experience
- **Brand fatigue**: over time, companies may become bored with their brands, or forget that they need to keep their edge on a regular basis.
- **Brand obsolescence**: a brand might become irrelevant by failing to appreciate the new technology or changes in

consumer habits and not noticing that the competitive set has evolved. As a result, they look dusty and old fashioned.

–   **Brand inconsistency:** frequent changes in creative leadership might result in changes of positioning that confuse the consumer.

While all the above are valid, in practice it is usually difficult to identify the main reason for the under-performance of a brand. That is why it is recommended to focus on the main financial and quant KPIs of the brand:

Table 9: Main KPIs of the brand and their evolution

	Year 1	Year 2	Year 3	Year 4	Year 5	TY Budget	TY LE	TY Plan	% LE vs Plan
FINANCIAL PERFORMANCE									
Volume									
Sales									
COGS									
A&P									
Margin									
Price/unit sold									
Margin/unit sold									
MARKETING INVESTMENT									
A&P/NS									
SOV									
SOV/SOM									
COMMERCIAL									
Weighted distribution									
CONSUMER									
Market share									
Spontaneous awareness									
% consumed more often									
Price index vs key competitor									

We analyze as well the performance (same KPIs) **by region** (to detect any difference in the brand performance and any possible drivers behind this discrepancy) as well as **by channel** (ex: comparative performance vs key competitors in hypermarkets, supermarkets, convenience stores, traditional trade, e-commerce and on-premise; analysis of promotional activities).

After the main weaknesses are identified in the financial and quant KPIs, we look at all relevant available research, studies and plans/analysis for our brand and key competitors (within last 3 years) in order to conduct a self-assessment of brand performance, positioning, equity and communication performance, based on recent qualitative research and expert opinions.

- Brand plans and brand reviews for last 3 years
- Brand equity monitoring or other equity/brand funnel, brand imagery scores
- Brand recruitment and brand retention analysis
- Qual research related to brand positioning and communication
- Ad hoc qualitative or desktop analysis of brand performance and brand issues
- Data/research related to the recent communication campaign performance
- Volumes and performance within the category for the last 10 years
- Nielsen market share (volume and value) evolution for the last 3 years within a category
- Net distribution, weighted distribution by channel
- Pricing vs. key competitors
- Price elasticity studies
- Shopper insight studies

We continue with a self-assessment of the Brand Identity, equity, and communication performance, based on recent qualitative research and management assessment, vs the current brand image:

- Is the brand identity distinctive & differentiating? If yes, why and how is that communicated to the consumer?
- How does the brand perform against key purchase drivers for consumers in the respective brand category and in the identified key moments of consumption for the brand?
- How do you differentiate between your recruitment and your retention strategy?
- Has the positioning strategy of the brand changed over the last 3 years? If yes, why has it changed and what has changed?

Using the Loosschilder-Schellekens model[23], we can enrich the self-assessment of the brand identity by analyzing the gap between brand reality and brand aspiration to help us better understand what are the key issues we want to address:

Figure 15: Bridging the gap between brand reality and brand aspiration

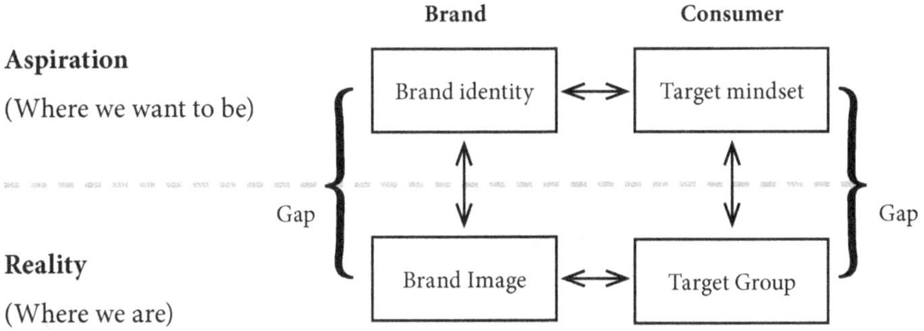

We then look at the **brand architecture** and the eventual sub-brands in order to analyze, for each sub-brand:

- Sales performance and profitability vs the main SKU
- Product difference vs. core quality SKU
- Price index vs. core Quality
- Strategic target
- Consumer proposition
- Role in brand architecture
- Role in company portfolio

Brand audits can be very powerful when done correctly. In our experience, you can reverse brand decline and start gaining market share in a matter of 1-4 years after the audit recommendations are implemented, depending on how strong the competition is.

4.3.2 Reviewing your brand strategy – "Do the right things"

Based on the successful completion of the Brand Audit, you can start reviewing your brand strategy.

Consumer segmentation

<u>Theoretical underpinnings</u>

Segmentation is based on the assumption that consumers differ from each other, but only to a certain extent, so that they can be grouped into relatively homogenous groups. The market heterogeneity concept has great managerial appeal, and segmentation models appear to do a great job in identifying useful groups that can be targeted with different (sub)brands and marketing tactics that optimize results. It has to be recognized, however, that every model is at best a workable representation of reality. Nobody can claim that segments really exist or that the distribution of heterogeneity is known. In fact, many marketing researchers believe there are no real consumer segments and that segmentation actually refers to managerial ways of analyzing data to enhance decision making. Which data points are analyzed matters as much as how they are analyzed. Having performed segmentations in more than 30 countries, I can say with high confidence that, whichever general segmentation approach you use, the most useful segmentations are those tailored and accepted by the country you are in. If done properly, segmentations remain important for defining a common language across organizations and for fine-tuning the strategy, as well as for training purposes, alignment within the organization, and portfolio management.

One-size-fits-all global segmentations based on demographics or psychographics are nearly always much less useful to decision-makers, no matter how inspiring and descriptive they appear. Market segmentation strategy is determined by the marketing manager's strategic view of the market. For different strategic goals, different segments may need to be identified in the same population, in order to be targeted with specific advertising goals.

In market research, segmentation is essentially a grouping task, and can be classified in two ways [23]:

- **A-priori and post-hoc approaches**. An a-priori segmentation approach is when the type and number of segments are determined in advance, before data collection. A post hoc segmentation is when the type and number of segments are determined on the basis of the results of the data analysis.

In practice, when performing a segmentation exercise in a big, global organization, it is very important that the local marketing and sales teams internalize the results and apply the recommended course of action. For these reasons, a hybrid approach a-priori/ post-hoc is used, meaning that a global segmentation passed down from the headquarters is adapted in-market to adapt to local cultural considerations, especially in the clustering procedure. Its effectiveness depends on the post-hoc clusterization, which needs to be done with the help of an experienced marketer in the region. On the other hand, the local variations should be linked back to the global model in order to produce relevant strategic insights for the brand. The goal of this approach is to determine associations between segmentation bases, for example between heavy users and light users of a brand by lifestyle segments, and between the strategic target and consumption pool.

- **Descriptive or predictive statistical models**. Descriptive models analyze the associations across a single set of segmentation bases, with no distinction between dependent or independent variables. Predictive models analyze the association between two sets of variables, where one set consists of dependent variables to be explained/predicted by the set of independent variables.

In practice, we used lifestyle hybrid (a-priori/post-hoc) descriptive methods, where the type and number of segments are predefined and then clusters of consumers are identified by brands based on their need-occasions by grouping together homogeneous consumers according to a set of measured demographic and psychographic characteristics. The clustering procedure can be data-driven or can be qualitatively driven, to identify clusters of consumers that are similar in terms of personality characteristics (values, activities, interests, and opinions) and behavior patterns. In practice, we used the qualitative approach, which tends to be better accepted than the quantitative one.

A consumer segmentation model is described below. In practice, for each brand, a limited number of consumer segments (max 10), need-occasions (max 14), and consumer clusters need to be created that are as homogenous as possible (max 5) in order to be manageable and distinctive. The importance lies in having different managerial implications for each type of heterogeneity assumption (i.e. targeting them with different communication strategies in different consumption modes) and the ability to predict actual or intended behavior. Otherwise, focus can be lost, and uncontrolled brand proliferation can be stimulated, rather than brand evolution.

Figure 16: Consumer segmentation map

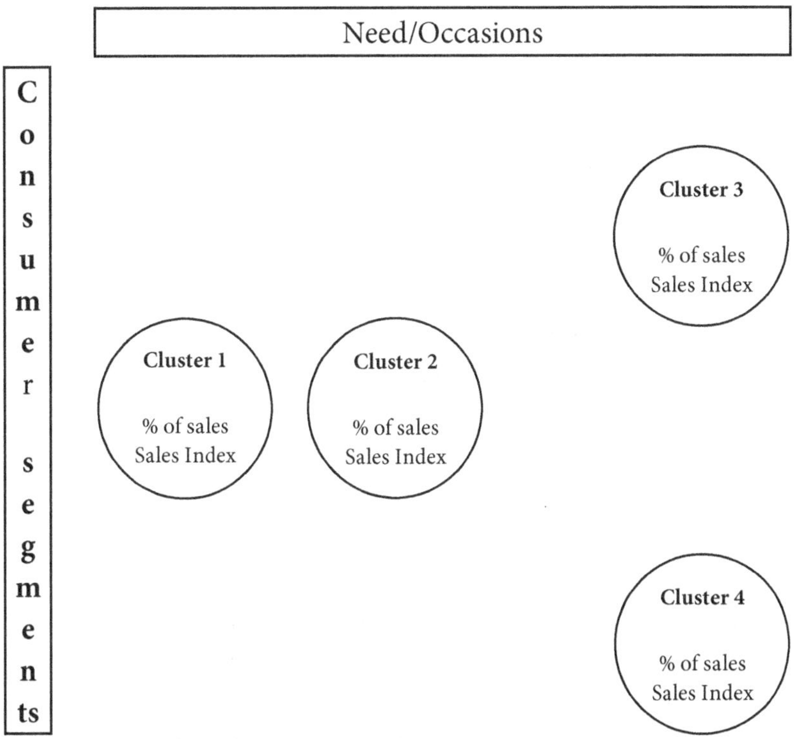

Byron Sharp[7] believes that in mass-market consumer product categories, segmentation and targeting are often empty exercises. In practice, it is true that consumption by consumer segments and need-occasions is quite uniform, and it is more a matter of management decision-making to determine the size, name, and characteristics of the clusters, as described above, than a pure statistical exercise. Sharp's argument is similar to the Fame Theory, which assumes that for mass-marketed brands, growth is a function of how many customers you can recruit, and that the best way to recruit as many consumers as possible is to advertise to as many people as possible. He argues that one of the common attributes shared by leading brands is that they have a long tail of light users, and the best way to acquire a long tail is to target everyone. This stands in stark opposition to the growth marketing theory.

On the other hand, Mark Ritson argues that segmentation and targeting are marketing essentials. He claims that no one can afford to reach everyone efficiently, due to budget limitations, and that without segmentation and targeting, strategy becomes dangerously nebulous and media dollars get sprinkled lightly everywhere instead of focused where they can do the most good.

My beliefs lie somewhere in the middle. My experience in the real world of marketing spirits taught me that mass media (especially TV) delivers the best results but it is often not practical either due to the brand budgets restrictions or due to media restrictions (in the case of the spirits industry and other restricted categories). As a result, the most efficient way for a major brand to use its advertising budget to acquire new customers and gain market share is to maximize effective reach within target consumers, either using media or non-media touchpoints. By increasing effective reach within target consumers, we will inevitably target more heavy users in the category. It is a question of maximizing probabilities (a Bayesian approach if you will), and not a precise science like *growth marketing*. The key issue is determining the most efficient way to use advertising dollars to acquire new customers, which is key to gain market share and benefit from economies of scale and S-curve effects. If possible (given the necessary budget, a decent creative campaign, and the absence of legal restrictions) mass media should be utilized, but it should be more heavily weighted towards heavy users in the category, to increase the probability of a sale. So, in my view, when targeting and segmentation are employed, they should be based on behavior, not demographics or psychographics. As Prof. Sharp points out, heavy users in a category tend to use several brands in the category. For example, heavy wine users tend to buy lots of different varieties and producers from different regions. Heavy single malt users tend to drink several types. As a consequence, you can focus on attracting new users from the segment of the population that is already active in the category.[7]

With the advent of big data and social media, many have proposed that *one-to-one* is a successor to market segmentation [25]. However, Wilson et al (2002) found that most one-to-one projects failed because of poor segmentation and Rigby et al (2002) argued that trying to implement CRM without segmentation is like "trying to build a hole without engineering measures or an architect's plan".

4.3.3 Marketing effectiveness fundamentals – "Do the right things right"

By now, we know how to determine an appropriate budget allocation by brand and set brand objectives. Assessing the major components of the marketing mix (or the touchpoints as they used to be called) is necessary because it can provide learnings at the company level, for best practice identification as explained in the Marketing Phronesis concept, and this sharing has been shown to improve methodology.

Before starting on your marketing effectiveness journey, you can begin with fourteen practical first steps:

Fourteen Practical First Steps for Marketing Effectiveness

1. Check your data

Analytical models are only as good as the data that they use (*junk in, junk out*, as they say). Before starting the marketing effectiveness journey, the marketers need to understand what the objective of the project is, be it maximizing revenue, market share, or profit, minimizing costs, and so on. Marketers must also determine what data they have that is relevant for the objective and if the data that they have is reliable (i.e. if the data they have makes sense from both a statistical and business point of view):

- What is your media budget? Does the size of your media budget justify doing a marketing mix modelling exercise?
- Does your data show that marketing investments are correlated with sales or market share? If not, what other data need to be considered (ex: price, competitor investments, social media, consumer research data, etc.)? Is this data available and reliable? Can you integrate and use data that you do not collect yourself, like weather, macroeconomic considerations, and industry statistics? What other internal data do you think is relevant for your objective?
- Can you easily access the data? Do you have a process to classify information that makes it easily accessible and standardized so that models can have consistent fields and values that are comparable and easy to work with?

In companies at the early stages of their data maturity (*beginners*), data management is very much a manual process, and marketers need to navigate through tons of invoices, excel files, and performance evaluation sheets, while making sure taxonomies are clear and consistent, and that ERP data is correct and clean.

More mature companies (*advanced*) automate data with APIs that can pull data from key systems and rely on methodologies for data cleansing and management.

Firms with highly skilled analytics and data teams (*best-in-class*) allow their analytics & data teams to access the raw data for specialized analysis.

2. Be focused on desired outcome and KPIs, not technology

Ask yourself: What do you or your management want to achieve? Is it revenue growth or cutting marketing spend to improve the bottom line? (usually, you can't do both). Or do you want to deliver more with the same marketing budget (increase ROI)? Or do you just want to create a marketing effectiveness culture in your organization (in which case, the technology is less important, and the mindset is more important).

What are the KPIs and the desired dashboards? How often do you want to collect the data? How often can you collect the data in practice?

Do you really need and have the resources (people, money, time) for a sophisticated analytics model, or can other tools or methodologies solve your problem (like the one explained in Chapter 4) ?

Do you need technology or a culture change, or both?

3. Choose your technology provider carefully

Before you choose a technology provider, I recommend going through a pre-design phase: make sure the potential providers understand your business and your industry, your point of view and your way of working, your business model (centralized vs decentralized, creatives vs implementers, etc.), how you make decisions (how much is heuristics vs how much is automated), governance, company culture, and what kind of information you use to make decisions. Each project is unique and has to be unique, designed for your specific needs and data availability and structure.

4. Understand your A&P budget split

Are you a media driven company or not? What about your competitors? Do they use similar tech solutions? If so, does their performance look better than yours or not? Is this difference likely to be sustained over the short-term vs long term? Do not forget that, with a few exceptions, marketing is not only about direct marketing, targeted ads and social media influencers. The fact that digital is easy to measure does not necessarily mean that you should maximize spend on digital, which usually produces strong short-term results without focusing on long term brand equity building. Brand identity and distinctiveness, semiotics (packaging, logo etc.), creatives, and traditional media play their own role in brand building and are usually at least as important as the digital.

5. Consider how technology IQ impacts decision quality

If it seems too good to be true, then it probably isn't. Ask for success stories and permission to speak with previous implementers. Consider price from an overall benefit and relative value, and not as an absolute value. In other words, if a solution can deliver 3-5% revenue growth or a 10% increase in marketing ROI at a cost of 2% of your marketing spend, then you might have an excellent deal even if it costs a fortune in absolute terms. On the other hand, if a solution costs very little money but does not improve your top or bottom line and does not help you learn something, you'll probably be worse off implementing it than the more expensive solution.

6. Recognize that marketing is not only about technology

Because it deals with humans, marketing is part science, and part art. It depends very much on context and is sometimes irrational. Experience and expertise are very important, especially if you want to excel at the subject. Marketing effectiveness is developing rapidly and has evolved beyond statistical methods into the realm of artificial intelligence: machine learning, algorithms, decision trees, neural nets, and the like. But as we discussed before, without human support, no system is able to drive the decision-making process.

7. Avoid mechanical number crunching statistics

Marketers today are pushed to crunch numbers on a weekly and monthly basis in order to demonstrate the ROI of their efforts. But these number-crunching approaches to decision-making are generally a waste of time and can even be misleading, because they focus on such a small timeframe. Check if your recommendations are internally consistent and supported by empirical evidence in similar markets. Use experimentation and case studies when you can.

I would avoid solutions that claim that their model can explain 99% of the data. There is not such a thing, nobody and no model is perfect, as humans are by nature irrational and sometimes unpredictable (although we would like to think otherwise). And nobody can predict the context in the future: what your competition will do, how the economy will evolve, when new trends and regulations will disrupt the industry, etc.

Even the most complex statistical models are simplified representations of reality. This is one reason why automated modelling without taking into consideration consumer perception can be so risky.

8. Consider scenarios recommendations directionally, not absolutely

Even if you have perfect confidence in your data, do not take the recommendation literally or do not over-interpret computer simulations. While empirical data should be a large factor behind your decision-making and marketing strategy and may at times dictate large shifts in your approach, it is important to also consider business and people realities at your organization. Strategy recommendations need to be understood and supported by the people at your organization in order to be implemented.

9. Recognize that raw data is an oxymoron

Accurate predictive models rarely need to be built on all the data that is available. On the other hand, if we could have access to all the possible data, everything would be correlated with everything and the noise would cover the signals. Therefore, you do not usually need zillions of data points for accurate modelling, and representative samples are more than enough. That is why statistics were invented, to use small samples to understand the larger population. Most Big Data has the same variables repeated over and over again, and you just need to pick a representative sample for more in-depth analysis.

10. Do not underestimate the role of creativity

It is as important as ever to create powerful, emotional content that changes consumer behavior.

11. Hire a marketing effectiveness sherpa

Even if you are an experienced alpinist, you cannot learn all there is about climbing Everest by yourself, and you probably shouldn't spend all your money on equipment without putting aside some money for the Sherpa as well, to support and guide you along the difficult marketing effectiveness journey ahead.

12. Do not confuse the possible with the plausible, and the plausible with fact

People are often confused about the difference between possible and probable. The number of things that are possible is infinite, but the fact that something is possible does not give us good reason for thinking it is true. You have a right to believe what you want (for example, that brands are built exclusively using rational persuasion), but this does not mean that people have an obligation to not say something to the contrary. If in doubt what works and what does not, use evidence-based marketing techniques, like case studies.

13. Create standard questions and questionnaire templates

Repeatability is key. Create standardized questionnaires in order to be able to run repeatable studies that answer your most pressing business questions. Constantly reinventing the wheel is inefficient and leads to inconsistent quality.

14. Be aware that response patterns in survey research differ from nation to nation

A 50% top 2 box score might be pretty good in some countries but pretty lousy in others. Employee and customer satisfaction research and NPS can easily fall victim to these cultural differences.

Knowledge and process recommendations

Start building an **effectiveness culture**, embracing data in a smart way that combines it with experience & creativity.

- Deploy marketing dashboards for lead brand-market combinations, and share them openly with sales and finance colleagues
- Roll-out marketing effectiveness trainings across the organization, and create marketing effectiveness ambassadors
- Build case studies to document successful decision-making
- Build an accurate A&P database for lead brand-market combinations and create benchmarks

Effective frequency

One of the key concepts in optimizing marketing effectiveness is effective frequency.

Imagine it is the end of the year, the best season of the year for many products and categories, and you are probably bombarded by advertising in all its forms and on all channels. Some brands seem to think that the more they advertise during this period, the more they will sell. But is this always the case, and if not, what is the most profitable communication planning strategy? This is an important question for advertisers, as it allows them to understand how to better allocate their budgets in order to optimize the equation between top-line sales, market share, and the bottom line. This is especially true in the current advertising environment, with the continued escalation of media costs and the increased push among advertisers not to spend more than necessary and/or sufficient, due to recession and/or consumption stagnation concerns. This produces an understandable pressure for more efficient buying.

To answer this question, we need to go back to some of the pioneers in statistics. Unsurprisingly, some pioneer companies like DuPont, General Electric, Procter and Gamble, General Foods and 3M, which were leading the industrial statistics field, are still leaders today. They developed better methods of experimentation in collaboration with academic institutions, especially after the 70s, when commercially available statistics software first appeared on the market. Some famous university research groups like Columbia's and Princeton's created methodologies that helped answer industry problems. This is an important lesson for today's advertisers...

But is the work of these pioneers relevant to the modern consumer, especially in the digital era? I think it is even more important because we can safely say that humans did not change too much in the last 50 years or so in terms of how they are influenced to buy stuff; it is just that having the right communication strategy became much more complex especially due to the increase in the amount and popularity of digital channels and the resulting media fragmentation and sophistication.

When speaking of *too much* or *too little* advertising, we need to talk about **reach** and **effective frequency**. Much of what is known about the effects of frequency can be traced to psychologically trained researchers who explored the subject in depth [16]. The business issue was simple:

- Is spending below a certain level a waste?
- Is spending above a maximum level likely to not produce results equal to the additional marketing cost?

Jakobovits and Appel (1965) were the first to suggest the concept of diminishing returns from greater advertising frequency, using **a life-cycle pattern of learning**. Learning increases with repetition, however, knowledge reaches a maximum and then declines. [16]

R.C. Grass of Dupont conducted a research study exclusively through TV advertising (1968) and found that the level of *attention* and *interest* generated in a subject when the audience was exposed to a commercial was maximized at 2 to 4 exposures to the commercial per month. He also discovered that generated attitudes are much more resistant to satiation effects than the recall of learned information. Based on this work, the concept of effective frequency at two or more exposures began to emerge [16].

Dr. H Krugman of General Electric suggested in 1972 that 3 exposures to a TV commercial might be the basic minimum number needed.

"We spend a lot of money on advertising repetition. Some explain this by noting that recall of the advertising will drop unless continually reinforced, while others note that members of the audience are not always in the market for the advertised product, but that when they are – the advertising might be there, so that there is no choice but to advertise frequently. So we can have advertising campaigns of equal magnitude, but based on quite different assumptions about the nature of the effect. Of course, these two views are apparently quite opposite. One says that the ad must be learned in the same way that habits are learned - by practice. The other says that at the right moment (when 'one is in the market') it just takes minimal exposure to achieve appropriate effects…" [16]

Krugman classifies the exposures as follows:

First exposure – *What is it?* – a cognitive response: understanding the nature of the stimulus, if only for the mental classification required to discard the object as of no further interest.

Second exposure - *What of it?* – an evaluative and personal response – is this product relevant for me? Some of it might occur during the first exposure if the respondent is highly engaged with the content, or if you can replay the content (as we can do today with YouTube videos). On 2nd exposure, the consumer starts to realize they've seen this before, and this is when the sale might occur.

Third Exposure - the true *reminder to buy*, but also the beginning of disengagement.

Krugman's work on the theory of advertising provides the most convincing psychological underpinning for the study of effective frequency.

McDonalds (1971), in a study conducted for J. Walter Thompson, demonstrated that scheduling for reach alone was inadequate because the one-exposure portion of the frequency distribution left a brand vulnerable to competitive activity [1]. He also demonstrated that, although effectiveness increases with frequency, it usually does so at a decreasing rate. Meaning that we need to **maximize effective reach** for a certain advertising budget in order to obtain the best sales response.

In 1965, **Ogilvy & Mather** looked at the relative effectiveness of daytime vs nighttime TV advertising, showing that:

- consideration of the frequency distribution of the reach is key in evaluating a schedule
- time of day effects are different depending on the type of product (ex: night time works better for toiletries)

In 1970, **D. Braun** of General Foods demonstrated that **media mixes work effectively**, showing some synergy effects. But he also asked some very important questions:

- Do the available measures of reach, average frequency, frequency distribution, and effective reach provide a benchmark for assessing the effectiveness of media mixes, or should relative media values be factored into the reach and frequency measures?

In 1974, a major advertising study [16] (with commanding shares of advertising in the respective categories) showed that:

- The probability of purchase increases with the share of category exposures, suggesting that brands should seek to dominate whatever medium they choose to be in
- Brands with longer purchase cycles (due to lower brand loyalty, smaller promo budgets, or relatively infrequent or seasonal consumption) are likely to benefit most from higher frequencies of exposure
- Very large brands behave differently from 'normal' brands in more competitive categories, as they likely do not have the problem of falling below the competitive share of voice.

In practice, this means that large brands (i.e. those brands that have at least twice the market share of the second-largest brand) can spend literally half as much on marketing as a % of sales as the average competitive brand. For example, a large brand can maintain a 40% market share with a 30% SOV, while a brand with a 5% share might require a 10% SOV. This means that exposure effectiveness for the big brand is almost 3 times as great as that of the smaller brand. Relative effectiveness = (40%/30%)/ (5%/10%)=2.67

Prof. Charles Ramond summarized the above as early as 1976: "Having decided what to say to whom, and how to say it, the advertiser must choose how often he would like each member of the target audience to receive his message. Given a limited budget, there is a necessary trade-off here. He may choose to reach more audience once, or a smaller audience more times. And given his sale or profit objectives, ideally, he would like to know the cheapest combination of reach and frequency to achieve those dollar goals." [26]

Because purchases are induced by communication, in practice you should be asking yourself these questions, in the following order:

1. How many times must an individual be exposed to my advertising message for it to have any effect on his subsequent behavior?
2. At what time interval must these exposures occur?
3. What number or portion of the target audience must I reach with the essential minimum frequency?
4. What other conditions might influence the results of this experiment?

After the 1970s, unfortunately, this subject did not receive much media attention, or at least studies were no longer made public because of the high costs involved and learnings obtained. When studies were conducted, the results went into private company files, helping to perpetuate media myths.

We can summarize all the above in a simple chart that shows the link between effective frequency and reach, as in the chart below first articulated by A. Achenbaum in 1977 [16]:

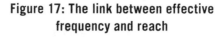

Figure 17: The link between effective
frequency and reach

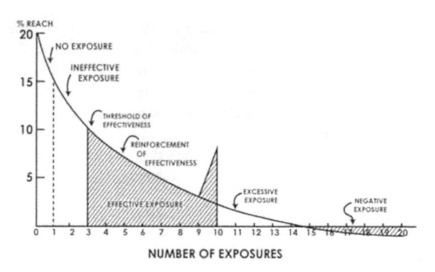

NUMBER OF EXPOSURES

Effective frequency (the range of exposure which is regarded as
desirable for advertising to be effective) and the resulting effective
reach concept passed the test of time. If there is too little exposure,
the advertising will fail to be noticed; if there is too much, the
recipient will be saturated, and the surplus will be redundant or
damaging [17]. Reach and frequency goals must be related to the
product purchase cycle.

Beyond effective frequency, of course, an effective comm plan
depends on many strategic marketing topics:

- Nature of product and category, based on consumer
  involvement with the category
- Brand objectives and lifecycle
- Brand maturity (new brand vs established brand)
- Engagement of consumers with certain touchpoints
- Brand market share and evolution of market share
- Brand loyalty

- Purchase cycles
- The relative cost of touchpoints and their reach
- Size of budget and ability to invest more/pressure to cut
- Synergies between different touchpoints
- The competitive level of spend and structure of spend
- Target consumer needs and touchpoint consumption patterns
- Distribution level
- Relative pricing vs main competitors and recent trends

Frequency depends on creative factors as well:

- availability and cost of creating content (this depends a lot on the type of content: TVC, videos, etc and formats: 30', etc)
- message complexity
- message uniqueness /stickiness
- campaign wear out
- new vs continued campaign
- nature of sell (image vs product)
- touchpoints used (number, amount, mix)
- the context in which the ad is placed

I believe that the answer to the question *is there such a thing as too much advertising?* is yes. For example, spending too much on digital to target the same people with very high frequency is counterproductive (especially if the brand has nothing new to say). You also need to beware of campaign wear out.

Marketing effectiveness for the beverage industry

Beverage companies do not always enjoy the luxury of having big, relevant data sets that tell them precisely what marketing activity sells and what doesn't; even in markets that have the data, companies struggle to find a way to improve their marketing effectiveness to generate optimal strategies.

Given the increased availability of data, the rise of digital media, and the heightened focus on marketing ROI, CEOs and CMOs across the globe are asking marketers to bring them the Holy Grail of marketing: a miraculous method that provides eternal youth for their brands and satisfaction to shareholders in the form of increased returns on marketing investment. The typical questions we get are: *Are we spending enough on digital? Or are we spending too much? Does TV still play a role and, if so, what is that role today? How can we better exploit experiential marketing? What message sells best? How important is creativity and distinctiveness? Where can we cut investments without hurting the bottom line? How can we increase our market share without increasing our investments?*

Our Marketing Effectiveness program tries to answer all the above questions, and is based on the following structure:

Figure 18: Marketing Effectiveness program structure

The problem with measuring marketing effectiveness is rooted in the very nature of marketing - i.e., dealing with consumers who are irrational (although, as Dan Ariely might argue, they are predictably irrational) [38]. It is difficult to assess performance and consumer choices within a context that is seemingly ever-changing. As a result, creating a general theory of marketing effectiveness, as many marketers have attempted to do, has its limitations.

A good reason to start a marketing effectiveness program is that managers tend to overspend on A&P. This may happen for different reasons:

- Most managers are risk-averse; they are reluctant to reduce advertising because of the potential adverse effects for sales and market share. Moreover, they are aware that once the budget has been cut, it is hard to get it restored.
- Managers often respond to competitive pressures as well as other market factors by increasing advertising. These actions are encouraged by agencies, who have a vested interest in increasing advertising billing
- Managers often overestimate the extent to which customers compare brands
- Managers tend to overreact to competitors, as they do not have the scientific evidence necessary to determine optimal advertising policy
- Declines in advertising effectiveness over the product life cycle may lead to overspending if a firm unreasonably maintains original sales goals or spending levels
- There is some indication that over-advertising could cost very little in forgone profit and might lead to appreciable sales gains (Tull et al.)

In the financial sector, machine learning is already being used to qualify loan applicants on the basis of risk, with a decision to grant the loan being automated. Unfortunately, we are still far from achieving this type of accurate predictive analysis within the marketing field, particularly within the beverage industry. As it stands, not all companies can afford the luxury of having access to Big Data analytics related to their consumers. If you are not GAFA or in financial services, telecom, or retail, or if you do not depend on eCommerce for a big chunk of your sales (like the fashion industry does, for example), you might find that your data is either incomplete or does not always make sense.

I started my marketing effectiveness journey five years ago, in collaboration with the renowned Professor Wagner Kamakura (at that time at Duke University). Together, we attempted to implement the most sophisticated statistical models in order to find the relationship between advertising and sales. We were hoping that, with mathematical rigor, the cleanest data available, and the smartest guys in the room, we would find the Holy Grail. However, after analyzing more than 2 years' worth of data (sell-out data in two channels, our own investment, and the competition's investment) the conclusion was that we could not find a mathematical relationship between the two. This is not to say that a relationship didn't exist, but that the way in which the spirits industry (and as a matter of fact many other industries) operates makes it almost impossible to build a mathematical model to measure ROI. Indeed, in this industry, digital media plays a relatively less important role than experiential and visibility touchpoints, which are much harder to quantify. Furthermore, there is limited competitor data available in channels that collectively represent about half of sales, making it difficult to build a reliable model.

We came to the conclusion that we needed to incorporate some measure of consumer perception into our model to complement the hard data.

For companies in which applying machine learning and/or econometrics to a large segment of exhaustive data is not an option, EFF-E Marketing and POINTLOGIC (a Nielsen company) propose a more holistic and adaptive approach. By combining consumer research with a strategic expert system, algorithms, and modelling, companies can take into account context to build a marketing effectiveness system. We found that comparative databases and benchmarking are as important to achieving a successful return on investment as pure mathematics. Building case studies, in particular, can help marketing teams navigate the market, as they often demonstrate how the market has responded to strategies in the past depending on the ever-changing context.

Below you can find our vision for a marketing effectiveness ecosystem:

Figure 19: Marketing effectiveness ecosystem

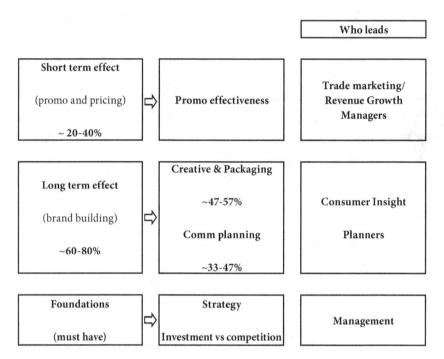

The solution that we found has two components:

- Recognize the fact that a marketing effectiveness **training** as well as comparative databases are as important as having a mathematical model as a decision support system, and that building successful **case studies** will help improve effectiveness.
- In order to build a best-in-class marketing effectiveness strategy, it is necessary to develop an intuitive, user- friendly **decision support system** that combines consumer research and strategic planning with real touchpoint cost data, algorithms and response curves to deliver a robust decision support system that is used to guide decision making

But to have a complete picture, let's have a look at the table above that summarizes my view on marketing effectiveness in the premium beverage industry, and is based on my own experience in running effectiveness projects as well as a meta-analysis of studies and literature on this topic.

It combines:

- **Short term effects**, mainly promotions and price management.

  o For promotions, the objective is to improve ROI by analyzing depth and width of promotions, optimizing last three feet or last click solutions (in the case of eCommerce/eRetail) to come up with a set of golden rules that can be applied going forward.

  o Price management is looking to optimize either sales, market share, or profit, depending on the broader company objective

- **Long term effects** are divided into two subcategories:

  o Creativity and packaging – creativity is potentially the most important part of the mix, depending on the category (level of consumer involvement, degree of maturity) and competitive context or potential for disruption. It can be measured by live testing, qual, online quant, or neuroscience

  o Comm planning – it is unlikely that even the most creative campaign in the world will turn a wrong strategy into a commercial success. That is why a solid decision support system must be put in place, together with a solid strategy (positioning, differentiation, objectives, consistency), proper training, benchmarking, and case studies. Comm planning has a dominant role in the brand's advertising and marketing communication strategy. Independent of the eventual solution in terms of how the brand's touchpoints mix is deployed, an understanding of the role and benefits of every touchpoint and its cost effectiveness in execution is fundamental to successful communications.

One of the studies mentioned above is the famous *The Long and the Short of It* by Binet and Field [15]. I have slightly adjusted downwards the short-term effect from the original 40% described in their study to 20%, to account for different life stages of the brand (more mature brands need more short term activities, while new brands, in particular craft brands that are increasing in importance, might rely more on emotional campaigns and less on price), and the fact that we only looked at the premium range, which by definition is less dependent on price.

How can we interpret this summary, as well as key takeaways of more than four years of work on the marketing effectiveness project?

1. **No Holy Grail (at least not in every industry!)**
    There is no one metric that encapsulates marketing effectiveness. Marketing effectiveness is more than just marketing ROI and KPIs. Although marketing alone cannot deliver business results, it remains the most important ingredient in the mix. Having a robust marketing system that is transparent (no black box) and puts together all the elements of strategy, execution, and creativity should be the main objective of each company. Creating a decision support system that is easy to understand and use, can be shared within the organization between marketing, sales, purchasing, and finance departments,

but takes into consideration as many factors as possible at a reasonable cost to the company (ideally less than 1-2% of A&P investment) is a must.

2. **Holistic view**
   We need to have a holistic view, looking at short vs long term objectives, context (competitive pressure, economic conditions, consumer trends, market disruptions), creativity vs reach, and quality of execution. We need to balance the need to explain the past with the need to forecast the future, and in doing so limit the number of KPIs to keep it simple.

3. **Culture first**
   Creating a culture of marketing effectiveness, using case studies, or business cases and breaking the silos within the company by sharing best practices and learning from failures might be the most efficient way to improve the marketing effectiveness.

4. **Do the basics right**
   Doing the basics right, like building a comparative database between brands in different countries or between the same touchpoints, is important to ensure you have a reliable data set to base decisions on.

5. **Strategic choices matter**
   For companies operating in multiple countries, switching investments from one country to another or from one brand to another within the same country portfolio might constitute a low-hanging fruit for success, before starting any marketing effectiveness program. Choosing the right KPI depends on strategy, and having the right strategy depends on a strategic assessment of the business that takes into consideration the consumer needs, life stages of the brand, competitive

positioning and pressure, ability to implement (route-to-market, relationship with wholesalers and retailers, and maturity of the organization). Having the right amount of innovation is also key: any brand could become obsolete if it does not bring new news on the market to stay relevant to the consumer.

Unfortunately, few companies are concerned with assessing marketing performance. Asking only about the performance of some element of the mix is not possible if context is not taken into consideration. The better approach to ROI is to identify the cost of achieving the brand's objectives and then play with the mix to reach them more economically [33]. As Tim Ambler says, *effectiveness precedes efficiency*, doing the right things even if not efficiently is better than efficiently doing the wrong things.

Marketing effectiveness can be judged by the extent to which the marketing plan improves the company's competitive position, i.e. profit and/or market share. But in practice:

–   We should not allow marketers to select the performance indicators _after_ the project has finished. In this way, they can show improvement only on those indicators that improved, and hide those that did not
–   We should not allow marketers to select vanity performance indicators, like number of likes, views and comments, which have no proven effect on performance.
–   We should use a better KPI than *performance vs previous years*

Marketing remains the most important ingredient in the mix that determines company success and value creation. Many companies have given up on finding the Holy Grail of marketing effectiveness, and more still are searching in vain by attempting to apply complicated mathematical formulas to a dataset that simply does not reflect the company's reality. I have come to the conclusion that building a Marketing Effectiveness ecosystem, with a dedicated decision support system that is easy to understand and use, is adapted to industry/category specificities and that can be shared within the organization between the marketing, sales, purchasing, and finance departments, and is supported by relevant training, benchmarking and case studies is the most important step in tackling effectiveness. This marketing system must be transparent and take into consideration as many factors as possible at a reasonable cost (ideally less than 2% of total A&P investment). Furthermore, the system must incorporate both long and short-term objectives, as well as account for context (competitive pressure, economic conditions, consumer trends, market disruptions, etc.)

Of course, all of this is easier said than done. For some companies with sufficient personnel, budget, and time, these decision-making systems can be developed and implemented internally. For others, external consulting services from companies that have the experience, strategies, and analytics already in place is the more cost-effective way to go.

Marketing effectiveness workshop

Marketing effectiveness has become top of mind for CEOs around the world for a very simple reason: it is defining the difference between winners and losers in the marketplace, and investors and stakeholders alike are realizing it and demanding a change. The objective is to get incremental results from marketing investment, creativity in the digital world, and pricing decisions and promotions in order to win the battle with the competition.

With marketing budgets as a percentage of revenues flattening or even declining, CMOs are investing in marketing technology. Marketing technology or Martech now accounts for almost one-third of marketing budgets in the US, while in-house labor investments lose share. But marketing leaders must demonstrate the business value of their efforts amid uncertain times.

The challenge is not to find a technology that automates internal processes to achieve efficiencies, but rather to train your team on a culture of efficiency that shapes the way your organization approaches marketing and sales. You can start by organizing a workshop with your sales & marketing team. Usually 20 people attend the workshop: marketing teams, including trade Marketing, but also CEO, CFO, Commercial Director, and Strategic Planners that are involved in improving overall organizational effectiveness

Organize a marketing effectiveness workshop with your sales & marketing team

The workshop has the objective to allow participants to understand the marketing effectiveness areas, explore the strategic importance of marketing effectiveness, and the tools available to build a solid knowledge platform. The participants should be able to acquire knowledge in few key areas:

Table 11: Marketing Effectiveness workshop structure

Introduction	Understand the two key areas of marketing effectiveness and the role of each of them
	Key take-outs from Marketing Effectiveness implementations in your industry

Key Steps in Marketing Effectiveness	Key challenges in implementing MEP
	10 practical first steps for marketing effectiveness
	What are we looking for when we start a MEP?

Models for Marketing Effectiveness & key takeouts	Marketing effectiveness test
	Main models for marketing effectiveness. Advantages and disadvantages

Marketing Effectiveness for beverage industry	Demonstration of a marketing effectiveness solution
	Case studies, examples
	Review the first results of the Marketing Effectiveness Test

The Marketing Effectiveness test

"The first duty of the business manager is to strive for the best possible economic result from the resources currently employed or available." – Peter F. Drucker

Improving marketing effectiveness is probably the most important element in increasing profitable growth. Yet when people talk about marketing effectiveness, it is not clear what it means and how it can be measured. Defining the right balance between short term and long-term objectives, the right priorities according to your strategy, and the right measures and areas of improvement is key.

The marketing effectiveness test is a diagnostic tool that has been developed by EFF-E Marketing Consultancy© (see Appendix 1). You need to answer 60 multiple-choice questions to measure your company's efforts in terms of marketing effectiveness. The tool, which can be used free of charge on our website, www.eff-e.com, generates a personalized report that benchmarks your organization against others and makes recommendations to help you improve your position.

After you complete the test, you will be able to benchmark how your company ranks on a Marketing Effectiveness scale.

Not started yet: Companies at this stage use last year's plan and adjust it slightly, depending on the attractiveness of new campaigns and other heuristic factors (like previous experience).

Beginner: At this stage, companies use some data to improve their marketing effectiveness in some channels

Good performer: At this stage, companies have integrated data across channels with a clear link to ROI/REMI or sales proxies

Best-in-class: At this stage, companies have real-time, dynamic optimization across channels and across the consumer's decision journey.

The tool generates a personalized report that makes recommendations to help you improve your effectiveness in each area analyzed, based on questions which cover the 10 different dimensions of marketing effectiveness: organization, promotions, price management, creativity & innovation, packaging, reach & touchpoints, targeting, portfolio management, strategy & resource allocation, and competitive investment.

It can be filled-in either collectively, with a group of experts in the above fields, or by an individual who has a very good broad view of all aspects of the organization's marketing efforts (including trade marketing).

The assessment takes about 1 hour to complete.

Key challenges in implementing marketing effectiveness programs

We see four big challenges that companies face when implementing Marketing Effectiveness programs:

1. First challenge is **data**. Handling data, data accuracy, and availability – from retail sell-out data to sell-in data and transactional data, it is already a challenge. But the real value is created by leveraging external data, like competitor data and consumer research, that can be combined with internal information to build an integrated data lake that can be used across the company.

2. The second challenge is what kind of **analytics** to use: from econometrics and marketing mix modelling to multi touchpoint attribution, to artificial intelligence, the choices are seemingly never-ending.

An even more difficult job is getting the **right skills**, either within the organization or by hiring an external consultant, to drill down into the data and find the real insights that can drive decision-making. On the other hand, do not expect that data alone will show you the way: raw data is an oxymoron, you need to start with a few hypotheses and then find the analytics that will enable you to gain the insights you need.

3. The third challenge is **cost**: how much should you invest in cost optimization as a percentage of your marketing spend? If you operate in multiple countries, you might consider a two-tier solution: a more sophisticated solution for big markets, and a lighter version for small and medium markets. Assuming your marketing effectiveness project delivers 3-4% in additional revenue, you can afford to spend about 1-2% of your marketing budget on a marketing effectiveness solution and still deliver a substantial increase in your margins.

4. But the most difficult challenge is to take the insights and **transform** the way the business operates, even if it will destroy company myths and well-known practices. You can change the business decision-making process from pure heuristics to a combination of heuristics and data-driven decision making, by following the three points above. This requires not only software implementation, but also training your people to operate in a different way, making them more accountable for their business results. This is a difficult process and may require you to hire externally as well as training existing employees, but it will be worth it.

5. You might need to appoint **a leader accountable** for your marketing effectiveness program, in every organization where this program is implemented. Define the scope and success

measures for your investments in order to foster the right skills and capabilities required to drive business results, and to set and manage expectations.

6. You might need to **combine financial measures with marketing KPIs** on your strategic dashboard. Build a clear connection between the leading indicators of marketing success, such as awareness, market share and price, with revenue and ROI.

Conclusions

We have concrete evidence, based on business results, of the superior brand performance that can be generated by designing best-in-class brand plans through touchpoint planning and creative delivery, and balancing short term and long-term objectives, as well as recruitment and retention goals, and being consistent over time. By supporting this framework with a Phronesis Marketing approach in terms of training and development of the marketing department, your chances of success in the marketplace can be maximized, even if your budgets are below your competitors' levels.

Regarding comm planning and buying, whether the client marketer is the decision-maker or delegates the role to a few agencies (usually one for media and one for experiential), it is difficult to achieve a genuinely integrated communication campaign for a brand. It is the question of prioritization: should clients prioritize the touchpoint strategy or the creative idea for the brand? If the former, then the agencies charged with the production of content are likely to complain that the mandated touchpoint mix does not suit their creative concept. If the *big creative idea* takes precedence, the media agency may despair at the cost or the time required [48].

In my experience, for global brands, since creatives are done at the central level in collaboration with 1-3 major markets for the brand, the only role of most marketing executives at the individual country level is to deploy the best strategy and touchpoint mix and ensure seamless execution. Therefore, the touchpoint mix has precedence in most markets except the priority markets, which usually account for 40-60% of the brand sales.

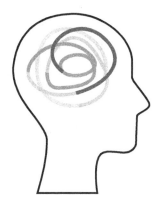

FIVE
Phronesis marketing

"Long years must pass before the truths we have made for ourselves become our very flesh." *Paul Valery*

"We are faced with a new kind of difficulty. We have two contradictory pictures of reality; separately neither of them fully explains the phenomena of light, but together they do." *Einstein*

In this chapter, we propose a new view on marketing effectiveness excellence, that answers the current challenges of modern marketing, based on a new interpretation of a century-old concept of phronesis. The goal is to help restore the credibility of the marketing community to improve marketing accountability while clarifying problems, risks, and possibilities we face in dealing with (sometimes irrational) consumers and societies we live in.

In advertising, consumer behavior has a dual character: rational, that can be captured by marketing laws and principles, and irrational, that can be managed through case studies and best practices. Just like in quantum physics, in advertising our strategies have no inevitability about them. But we can increase the probability of success by better understanding the underlying marketing models. And we need to overcome the phenomena of marketing experts not learning about their past failings.

Establishing a structural marketing skills training path during the marketers' first years in the company is a must. It is surprising how many marketing teams do not have a structured skills development program. If you do not have such a program, you need to create one, and it should incorporate at a minimum basic functional marketing skills (that can be developed internally), basic marketing leadership skills (that can be tailored to the particular skills needed), and required functional on-the-job experience. More about this in Chapter 7.

Recently, a lot of talk has been centered around marketing effectiveness. We need to give kudos to Les Binet and Peter Field (*The Long and the Short of It, The Link Between Creativity and Effectiveness* and *Effectiveness in Context*), Byron Sharp (*How Brands Grow*), Mark Ritson, WARC, and many others who have popularized this subject in the wider marketing community.

The main topics in modern marketing were summarized in a recent WARC webinar [2]. The main themes of discussion are summarized below:

o The advance of **performance marketing** (driven by social media and data) together with the demise of brand advertising result in a collapse of the funnel. Differences between brands and activations have become blurred. Focus on persuasion, rational appeals, always-on communication, and personalization creates inconsistent, undistinctive, me-too creative strategies.

o   There has been increasing recognition of the **role of creativity in a low-attention economy**. Emotions are key, as they drive long-term effectiveness and help build memory structures

o   We need to **balance performance with brand building**, short term with long term, and targeted reach with broad awareness.

Why is it so difficult to come up with a general theory of marketing effectiveness that responds to the above challenges?

To answer this question, we were inspired by the work of Bent Flyvbjerg, currently Professor at Oxford University [18]. Prof Flyvbjerg presents a new interpretation to a century-old approach to the social and behavioral sciences, called phronesis.

Aristotle, in arguing that natural and social science are and should be different ventures, discusses the three intellectual virtues: episteme, techne, and phronesis. *Episteme* is found in the modern word *epistemology*, or the theory of knowledge, and *techne* in *technology*. It is indicative of the degree to which thinking marketing today has allowed itself to be dominated by natural and technical science that we do not even have a word for the other intellectual virtue, phronesis, which was considered the most important one by Aristotle.

Based on Prof. Flyvbjerg's work, we propose a new approach that will balance *scientific advertising* or *performance marketing* (i.e. a set of persuasion and rational rules that improve short term performance but not necessarily long-term brand building) with the challenges of measuring *creativity*, using case studies and best practice sharing, approach that we call *Marketing Phronesis*.

While recognizing that there are some general marketing laws that are useful to create a marketing epistemology, we are not trying to emulate the natural sciences and create a kind of general theory, but rather propose a broader, holistic view, in which we move beyond the purely analytical or technical to put to work and recognize the strengths of marketing as a social science using case studies as the base of Marketing Phronesis. The difference between marketing and natural sciences seems to be too constant and too comprehensive to be a historical coincidence. Even relatively new natural sciences, like meteorology, which also struggle with especially complicated objects of study, are moving into predictive theory, while marketing, despite huge amounts of research, is lagging behind.

The Marketing Phronesis concept is explained below:

Table 12: Marketing Phronesis concept – five levels of marketing excellence

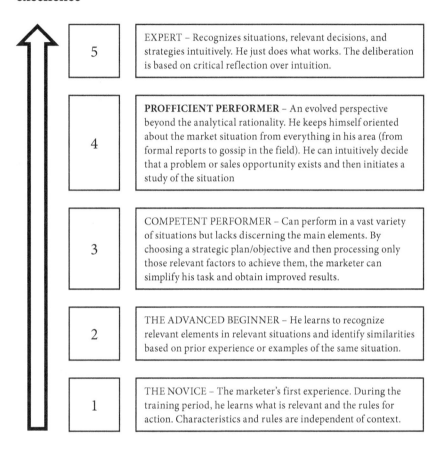

5	EXPERT – Recognizes situations, relevant decisions, and strategies intuitively. He just does what works. The deliberation is based on critical reflection over intuition.
4	**PROFICIENT PERFORMER** – An evolved perspective beyond the analytical rationality. He keeps himself oriented about the market situation from everything in his area (from formal reports to gossip in the field). He can intuitively decide that a problem or sales opportunity exists and then initiates a study of the situation
3	COMPETENT PERFORMER – Can perform in a vast variety of situations but lacks discerning the main elements. By choosing a strategic plan/objective and then processing only those relevant factors to achieve them, the marketer can simplify his task and obtain improved results.
2	THE ADVANCED BEGINNER – He learns to recognize relevant elements in relevant situations and identify similarities based on prior experience or examples of the same situation.
1	THE NOVICE – The marketer's first experience. During the training period, he learns what is relevant and the rules for action. Characteristics and rules are independent of context.

Based on the model described above, I have identified five levels of marketing excellence. The first three levels are based on rational skills, creating the epistemological and technical basis of marketing. These first levels are based on a rule-based choice of goals and decisions after reflecting on various alternatives. In practice, these are taught in business schools in the form of *product, price, place* (or *distribution), promotion* and *advertising principles,* of course with elements of social media and direct marketing. This allows the Novice to have his/her first marketing experience in a company.

In the 2nd and 3rd level, Advanced Beginner and Competent Performer, the marketer learns about marketing strategy, strategic planning, portfolio management, segmentation, positioning, and targeting, and starts to implement all these concepts in real life, achieving real-life experience. At these stages, he still lacks the capability to discern the main elements of how marketing actually works. By choosing a strategic plan or objective and then only processing those relevant pieces of information to achieve them (about competition, trends, channels, categories, role of creativity and innovation, etc.) but also practical limitations of implementing plans (like budget constraints, running promotions and price management, availability of relevant talent and creative solutions), the marketer can simplify his task and obtain better and better results. At the peak of Level 4, the marketer has learned all the marketing principles, compares different ways of achieving the same results, and records his experience. When one method invariably proves the best, that method becomes a fixed principle. From mail order to e-commerce and CRM, everything is traced down to the dollar. One ad is compared to another, one method with another, headlines, settings, sizes, pictures, and videos are compared. To reduce the cost or to increase the ROI, every dollar counts, every half of a percentage of effectiveness translates into money won or lost. When ROI calculations are impossible (which is very often the case), countries, regions, or towns are compared with each other to achieve the best cost per dollar of sale or cost per customer.

To jump to Level 4, the marketer needs to perform a qualitative jump from the first 3 levels, replacing rule-based thinking with context and intuition based on experience. At these levels, the marketer has developed an evolved perspective beyond analytical rationality. He keeps himself oriented about the market situation (from formal reports like qual and quant market research, retail audits, etc.) and starts to quantify the short- and long-term effects of advertising, as well as understanding the limitations of the rational approach. Studying how advertising works could have a place in Stage 4 or even 3.

At Level 5, the Expert level, the marketers recognize situations, relevant decisions, and strategies intuitively, and understand how marketing works. They just do what works, in a similar way that a chess Grand Master decides how to move the pieces on the chess table. This does not mean that they do not think consciously, nor that they always do the right thing. Their deliberation is based on critical reflection over intuition.

The goal of Marketing Phronesis is to contribute to the ongoing dialogue between marketing professionals rather than to generate ultimate, unequivocally verified formulas. This is what I call a *marketing dialogical attitude*, with the development of case studies or best practices looking at short, medium- and long-term effects, similar to the ones developed by Field, Binet and Mark Ritson, but using more concrete cases. Many believe that case studies do not provide a solid basis for marketing decision-making because they rely on a handful of experiences as opposed to a broad set of data points favored by the scientific method [1]. But if we go back in history, we find many examples of great innovations that were thought up based on a small data set, like Galileo's rejection of Aristotle's law of gravity, which was based primarily on a conceptual experiment and later on of a practical one (the famous tower of Pisa experiment). Carefully chosen experiments, cases, and experiences were also critical to the development of Newton, Einstein, Darwin, and Freud's theories. As W.I. Beveridge observed, "more discoveries have arisen from intense observation of very limited material than from statistics applied to large groups" [18].

If case studies are so useful, why aren't they being used? Well, for four obvious reasons:

o Writing case studies is tedious work: it requires not only an expert, independent view but also collaboration between multiple stakeholders and recollection of facts that might have been forgotten in the organization

o Spreading case study learnings is difficult too. Due to the confidential nature of the information, companies might not be willing to share it publicly

o *Not invented here syndrome*: the reluctance of marketers to learn from each other

o The phenomena of marketing experts not learning from their past failings, perhaps because they refuse to accept their failures.

The good news is that, based on my experience, with careful, diligent work, all four obstacles can be overcome.

The marketing industry never has been, and probably never will be, able to develop the type of explanatory and predictive theory that is the ideal of natural science. What works for finance, IT, and even sales does not work for marketing. Context and judgment cannot be put in a theory. But what marketing can do is to reinterpret the Aristotelian concept of phronesis and create case studies, based on intense observation of consumers, over a longer period of time, in order to draw lessons.

HOW TO CREATE A PHRONESIS MARKETING LEARNING CULTURE BY SHARING BEST PRACTICES

People do not share experiences spontaneously. Creating a sharing experience must be nurtured through a network of communities and experts that work together to create a sharing and learning culture. The main idea behind Best Practice Sharing (BPS) is to create both a business intelligence and emulation within the organization with highly contributive topics to help local teams bridge performance gaps and train them to become better in their field of activity. Similar to Lord & Thomas' *Record of Results* database of results from previous campaigns presented in Chapter 1, your Best Practice Program will help you reduce guesswork, thus increasing the effectiveness of your marketing spend.

A secondary objective is to achieve cost efficiencies by harmonizing processes and promoting innovation.

Staff expertise, motivation, and loyalty are additional expected outcomes, by creating a bigger sense of community and increasing the number and quality of exchanges outside the usual hierarchies. If you do not already have a BPS culture within your organization, and/or the *not invented here* syndrome is overwhelming, you need to create a step-change to align stakeholders against this approach in order to benefit from the advantages of BPS.

The BPS expert community must be visible and widely known by everybody and aligned with the existing management framework. The legitimacy and power of a functional community depends on the choice of its members. They must have demonstrated peer-approved expertise in the discipline and be able to think *outside the box*. In practice, the expert community enables the identification and generalization of best practices, the exemplarity and impartiality of its production being essential to get the commitment of both community members and management. A strong communication campaign should support the BPS approach, so that the work is totally transparent to the whole organization, including top management.

The BPS roadmap:

- Identifies impactful topics and prioritize them
- Leverages what already exists in the organization
- Clarifies governance and builds the IT infrastructure (organization and resources), combining a top-down and bottom-up approach
- Plans to recognize and celebrate success through awards and internal communication, inclusion in annual development review, bonus calculation, and career path

Table 13: BPS organization

	Objective	Criteria for selection	Examples
Priority topics	-Reinforce strategic objectives of the company -Develop competitive advantage and build leadership	-Strategic fit with the company's objectives -Measurable impact on short and long-term performance, with clear KPIs -Differentiation potential and innovation	Structure by function: -Marketing -Commercial -HR -IT -Finance -Operations
Norms and references	Develop a common way of working and common language	Generalization potential (limited rework, easily understandable)	-Performance assessment -Brand equity monitoring -Brand plans
Operational topics	Share operational efficiency levers	Procedures	-Salesforce incentives -Brand activation tactics

A global virtual library needs to be created, with unique access points and rights, a clear taxonomy (ex: brand, lifecycle, size of market, function etc.) and collaborative features (i.e. possibility to be liked and shared). In practice, not all markets are comparable in size or complexity, and you might need to group them by budget size or type of market (emerging vs developed), or degree of sophistication.

This database would allow all marketing and branding teams to base their strategic decision on prior performance and case studies, thus offering them an incredible advantage as compared to the current status quo.

Examples of priority topics:

Commercial

Shopper Insight

Category Management

Pricing and Trade Terms

Key Account Management

Off-trade Promotions

On-trade Promotions

Marketing

Generating Consumer Insights

Optimizing Resources across 360 Touchpoints

Big Events/Festivals

Regular Small Event Optimization

Product Launch

Digital Media

Traditional Media Optimization

CRM

Agency Briefs and Evaluations

Transversal

Best re-use of a previous best practice

Learnings from past failures

Conclusions

Creating a BPS community and process will connect people and expertise, provide a global overview of competencies and know-how, promote mobility, align market approaches and processes, and build a common language that will foster practice sharing and promote excellence.

 **CASE STUDIES**

Absolut vodka - the creative, culturally relevant brand

Without doubt, Absolut Vodka, one of the most successful brands in the spirits industry, owes its fame to the most creative, culturally relevant and long-lasting campaign ever created for a spirit brand. The ABSOLUT VODKA advertising campaign launched in 1980, has continued to run ever since and has been recognized as one of this century's greatest by the American trade publication Advertising Age and the American Marketing Association's Marketing Hall of

Fame, to name just a few. Absolut advertising is celebrated not just for its longevity but also for its creativity and ingenuity.

The brand had humble beginnings, introduced in 1979 to the US market as an imported vodka from a country not known for its vodka. But the brand did not remain humble for long. Absolut has achieved sales totaling over 2 million cases in only 10 years and by 1985 became the single largest imported vodka in the US. Americans became familiar not only with the product and the name but with the advertising, promotion, and publicity campaigns. Absolut has become, literally, a household word. How did this marketing phenomenon happen?

The answer begins, as it does for all successful beverages, with what is in the bottle and the bottle itself. Absolut has its origins in the grain fields and the clear streams of Sweden and owes its taste to its superb distillation process. The tradition of distilling in Sweden goes back almost as far as alcohol distillation itself. It was L.O. Smith (1836 – 1913), a Swede, in fact, who more than a century ago perfected the process and who first produced a spirit that bore the name Absolut. His aim was to improve public health through a better product, *Absolut rent Brännvin* or *Absolutely Pure Vodka*, launched in 1879.

But Absolut's phenomenal success in the U.S can in large part be attributed to the selection of Carillon Importers as the brand's U.S marketer. Absolut Vodka would arguably not have seen its present success without Michel Roux, the president of Carillon, and his vision of a product that would not only fit the most sophisticated American lifestyle but would actually help to shape this lifestyle. That vision also led to the selection of TBWA, a remarkably creative, international agency, to develop advertising campaigns for the brand and act as a public relations counsel.

Based on this experience, Absolut executives believe to this day that individual vision is a necessary element of success. One person, presumably the chief executive officer of the importing company, must drive the campaign. He or she must demand - and receive-creativity from every person and organization involved, but that person must understand the brand's remarkable potential, make the necessary commitment of resources, and lead the charge.

The 1980 ABSOLUT VODKA campaign is one of the 10 top campaigns that relied exclusively on print media. Then and now, the campaign centers around the unique bottle (inspired by Swedish medicine bottles and the first liquor bottle without a paper label) with a two-word caption starting with the word ABSOLUT. The first ad "ABSOLUT PERFECTION" had a distinctive wit that redefined alcohol advertising.

Figure 20: ABSOLUT PERFECTION:
"© The Absolut Company"

Figure 21: ABSOLUT WARHOL "© The Andy Warhol
Foundation for the Visual Arts. Used by The Absolut
Company under exclusive license. ABSOLUT is a
registered trademark of the Absolut Company"

Figure 22: ABSOLUT GENEVA: "©The Absolut Company"

Figure 23: ABSOLUT CAMERON: "©The Absolut Company/David Cameron"

ABSOLUT CAMERON.

Michel Roux made a defining decision in 1985: he commissioned the late Andy Warhol to paint the Absolut bottle. The success of Absolut Warhol, as both a work of art and an advertisement, led to further commissions and ultimately, to an invaluable, unique element of Absolut's image: patron of American artists, composers, interior designers, fashion designers, and others. This broad association with the arts fit perfectly with the other elements of the Absolut image.

But Andy Warhol was not only a famous artist who commented on mainstream America through his art. He was what we would call today a *mega influencer* through The Factory, his New York City studio, the hip meeting place of artists and musicians, and famed for its groundbreaking parties. David Bowie, Debbie Harry, Grace Jones, Madonna, Liza Minelli, Lou Reed, Keith Richard, and Mick Jagger were among his parties' attendees.

Then Absolut fashion commissions began: when Absolut Versace appeared in international editions of Vogue in April 1997, media coverage followed. Designs by the biggest names in the industry, images by legendary photographer Herb Ritts, top models standing half-naked in arctic temperatures - the event was definitely one-of-a-kind. Two months later, all expectations had been exceeded - half a billion people all around the world had seen the pictures, either in the original insert, in editorial articles, or through TV coverage.

Other collaborations include Jean Paul Gaultier, Marc Jacobs, Gucci, Tom Ford, Stella McCartney, Alaya, and images in collaboration with famous photographer Helmut Newton.

By 1989, The Absolut fashion commissions had taken the form of an annual collection, and the moment was right for something dramatically new. That *something* was a glistening dress by designer Anthony Ferrara made entirely of fine 18-Karat gold links. The Absolut name in sterling silver was applied to the bodice. If it were for sale, this one-of-a-kind dress would carry a retail price of USD 532,000. Spectacular? Of course. This dress would be made available as an attraction at fashion shows on behalf of charities. It has now been featured, with other Absolut designs, in fashion shows throughout the U.S. -- always to raise funds to aid the homeless, the hungry and others in need. As such, the gold dress has raised considerably more money for good causes than it cost.

Then, in January 1992, Carillon Importers began its most extensive advertising campaign in support of Absolut Vodka yet, which combined two of the key elements of the brand's personality: the arts and the support of worthy causes. The concept was ambitious: an established or emerging artist from each of the 50 US states would be commissioned to capture the spirit of his or her state in a work of art using the image of the Absolut bottle. Their work would be reproduced in a full-color, full-page ad in USA Today, a national daily newspaper. The campaign would be called Absolut Statehood. The work would be published with artist biographies every other Thursday for approximately two years - in alphabetical order by state. A limited edition of four hundred 27 x 34 inch lithographs of each artwork would be published. Of these copies, 300, numbered and signed by the artist, would be sold to the public for $300 each. All the proceeds of these sales would be donated to the Design Industry Foundation for Aids (DIFFA), a national foundation which distributes grants to local organizations fighting AIDS in communities throughout the U.S. Knowing that these works of art would be seen as newsworthy both nationally and at the local level, Carillon undertook an ambitious, comprehensive statewide publicity campaign.

This landmark campaign has resonated beyond US borders. The Absolut Statehood artworks also appeared in the international edition of USA Today and created a stir particularly in Europe and Asia. Several Absolut Vodka distributors worldwide took advantage of the campaign by copying the concept in their own country. Absolut Statehood demonstrated what could be achieved by tailoring creativity to individual markets. Since then, the brand image has been built from the ground up in each market, with the quality of the product and its Swedish origin as the foundation. Absolut's marketing strategy can be explained in two words: consistency and integrity.

In 1993 Seagram (at that time the number 1 spirits & wine company) was granted the distribution rights for Absolut Vodka, another important milestone in the brand's global success. And in 2002 Absolut was acquired for 6.8 billion dollars by Pernod Ricard.

Apart from content creativity, Absolut is also famous for its innovative, consistent and rigorous use of touchpoints:

Product placement - Another milestone in product placement was reached in the hit HBO program, Sex and the City, in 2003. Sex and the City changed the dynamics of the drinks industry in the US, promoting sophisticated cocktails to a wide audience. Who can forget when actor Jason Lewis, who played the handsome toy boy who brought out Kim Cattrall's softer side – became the star of an Absolut vodka ad in which he poses with just a bottle of spirits to hide his modesty. The fictional campaign has proved so popular that fans turned up in real bars and ordered the drink he was advertising: Absolut Hunk.

Ultimate bars - Like the bar situated at 2,100 meters in the Austrian Alps or the vodka bar in Chicago which featured a 4-meter chandelier made of 336 empty bottles of Absolut Citron.

Unusual billboards - Like the 4 by 6 meter billboard featuring 600 kilos of fresh fruit at the Covent Garden Piazza in the heart of London. The Absolut bottle was made out of lemons, the halo of light was formed with mandarin oranges, the background was a patchwork of limes, and the headline was written out in grapefruit. The fruit was replaced daily to keep the poster fresh and boxes of fruit were provided for admirers. The billboard was a success with both the media and the animals in the nearby zoo that were given the discarded fruit.

Drinkspiration – Absolut is responsible for the creation of the largest app for drink recipes, in 5 languages, based on vodka and other spirits as well as non-alcoholic options, complete with stunning images and videos

Absolut Akademi - An education program featuring world-renowned bartender conventions.

Absolut Design - A traveling exhibition of artworks from different Absolut campaigns. The *Absolut Design* campaign famously broke new ground in furniture design due to its collaboration with artists like John Saladino, Adam Tihany, Mario Buatta, and Dakota Jackson, with furniture creations ranging from avant-garde to elegant simplicity.

Absolut Cuisine - Recipes from the world's famous restaurants and chefs featuring at least one tablespoon of Absolut as a flavor intensifier.

P.O.I. (**Point of Image**) concepts built in collaboration with key markets, creating a global Point of Sales Buy Book since 1997 that set the standards of quality POS.

Creative gift box designs and limited editions – Every year Absolut launches two Limited editions (one for summer, one for winter) which collectors all over the world fight for.

Today, Absolut Vodka is still the number one premium vodka in the world, selling about 11.3 million cases.

Jägermeister – the tactical genius

Another success story in the spirits industry took a completely different path to Absolut's. It is less about artistic creativity (it has not produced any famous creative campaign) and more about tactics and aggressive sales techniques.

Jägermeister is a German bitter (technically, a half-bitter), known for its unique formula consisting of 56 ingredients and an unmistakably strong flavor (*love it or hate it*) and weird name. It was created by Curt Mast in 1934 in Wolfenbüttel, when he concocted a new version of the traditional herbal liqueurs that had been used medicinally for ages. He called it *Jägermeister - master hunter* - and, according to the brand tradition, intended it to be "a toast with which every hunt would begin and end."

Its masculine square green bottle was designed to be sturdy. The logo, inspired by the story of Hubert, the patron saint of hunters, is a stag with a glowing cross hovering between its impressive antlers.

In post-war Germany, Jägermeister was a sleepy little brand that you would drink as much for medicinal reasons as for taste-related ones. Although Jägermeister began gaining success when it began experimenting with sports team sponsorships in the 1970s, the real success was achieved by Sidney Frank in the US.

Sidney Frank, who married the daughter of Lewis Rosenstiel, founder of Schenley Industries, the largest American distiller and spirit importer at the time, rose to the company presidency and was forced out in a family dispute in 1970. He started his own company, Sidney Frank Importing, in 1972, with his brother and secretary. He started by supplying Japanese restaurants with Gekkeikan sake, but the first years were not easy, and he sold property and art to keep the business afloat.

Frank was looking for something to import when he first tasted Jägermeister in 1972 in New York. "I was looking for anything that had a niche," he told *Inc.* magazine [30], and he had a hunch Jäger did ("there were a lot of Germans around the country"). A year later, Frank was introducing it nationally, although it was not an immediate hit. In 1974 he sold only 600 cases.

In the 1980s, Jägermeister became popular with college students in Louisiana and Frank promoted it heavily, advertising it as the best drink in the world, turning a specialty brand into a mainstream success.

In 1985, an article was published in the *Baton Rouge Advocate* about the brand's hyper-popularity among Louisiana college drinkers. It tasted "like a mixture of root beer and Vicks Formula 44D cough syrup" according to the author, with a hint of liquid Valium."There were rumors it contained opium, that it was an aphrodisiac. It does not contain opium — it is not even particularly highly alcoholic, but it contains lots of sugar - but Frank turned the rumors into a viral marketing campaign, distributing thousands of photocopies of the article across New Orleans bars. Sales skyrocketed. Soon after, he introduced the new drink with a weird name using attractive Jägerettes in minimal clothing shooting liquor into men's mouths with a spray gun. Frank noticed that a well-trained Jägerette would be able to sample 80% of consumers in a bar. This aggressive sales technique is now prohibited in many countries, but it was allowed at the time. Jägerdudes were added later on too [30]. Then, after Red Bull was invented in 1987, the Jägerbombs — a Red Bull/Jägermeister upper/downer cocktail — became a pre-party staple, known for getting you energized and also for getting you drunk, especially in the famous after-ski parties in the Austrian Alps.

To increase Jägermeister's visibility in the bar and make it more drinkable (warm Jägermeister is hardly bearable), he came up with an innovative tap machine, which kept the spirit ice-cold (an ideal pour is below zero) without hiding it away in a freezer. The fact that neither strategy seems particularly innovative today is a testament to their success, although to this date the best tap machines are still made by Sidney Frank (the high percentage of sugar in the drink clogs the pipes in a less advanced tap machine).

Changing consumer tastes, restrictions in alcohol advertising, and cheaper alternatives like Fireball cinnamon whisky had a big negative impact on Jägermeister sales. Today, its current mission is to increase the drink's quality perception by appealing to consumer desire for craftsmanship: Jager is being re-introduced to the craft-loving crowd, emphasizing the 56 ingredients, the one-year aging process, 90-year-old recipe, and the 383 individual quality checks per batch. It is also attempting to step beyond its reputation as a party drink to become an old-school digestive moment of consumption, a staple at the routine barbecue with friends, as well as a must-have in fancy cocktails.

Jack Daniel's – deconstructing a strong personality

Whisky brands, like people, have personalities, which can make or break them in the marketplace. Jack Daniel's is one of the strongest and most recognizable personalities on the market, and it is made of many things – its name, its packaging, its colors, the style of its advertising, and the story behind the brand.

Every Jack Daniels ad is a contribution to its brand image, and it has been consistently projecting the same image despite changing its agency and marketing directors. The intangibles account today for 80% of the value of the brand.

As experts in the drinks industry know, whisk(e)y is the spirits category most driven by image (when talking about American and Irish whiskey, you spell it with an 'e', while Scotch and all other types of whisky are spelled without an 'e'). As Ogilvy used to say:"

I have always been hypnotized by Jack Daniel's. The label and the advertising convey an image of homespun honesty, and the high price makes me assume that Jack Daniel's must be superior" [31]. David A. Aaker claims that "Jack Daniel's whisky has drawn upon its Tennessee background to create a personality that reflects the pace and flavor of backwoods Tennessee culture. The result is an "authentic" position and an opportunity to develop links to customers". [32]

So far, no single whisky brand can face the Jack Daniels challenge, because it is harder to attack a brand personality than a functional benefit. Jack Daniels is the No. 2 whisky in the world, behind Johnnie Walker. Brown Forman, the parent company of Jack Daniel's, is one of the leading spirit companies in the world. In only 20 years, they went from being a largely American brand (in 1992, only 6 countries were selling more than 100,000 cases) to an international sensation.

At its core, Jack Daniels has its **brand identity**: the authentic masculine badge. Its personality can be described as quietly confident with lack of pretense, laid-back, Southern-leisure with a gentle sense of humor, and of course, a hint of rebellion. It has very traditional **values and emotional benefits**: integrity, honesty, trustworthiness, independence, craftsmanship, pride, consistency, coolness, camaraderie. Its advertisements highlight friendships and respecting the past, relying on small-town values and offering a pause from a hectic world.

Its **product features** and semiotics are its distinctive squared bottle, the black & white label, *Lynchburg TN (pop 361)* which creates a sense of scarcity, it's proud badge as *America's oldest registered distillery since 1866*, its unique, unchanged distillation process that gives its distinctive taste, the use of cave iron-free spring water, the Tennessee dry country image, and of course *Jack*.

With this carefully constructed personality, Jack Daniels manages not only to appeal to male consumers but to new premium whisky drinkers, which are mostly female.

Due to the increasing influence of popular culture, mainly driven by the American movie industry, successful TV series and docu-dramas such as Mad Men, Boardwalk Empire, and Moonshiners have proven to be great promotional vehicles for the US whiskey. They also used the Frank Sinatra image as a celebrity endorsement.

Jack Daniel's is also famous for its very consistent **art direction** (black & white colors, heavy use of fonts and mix of text, very identifiable symbols of **American culture**, widely shared across regions and audiences.) It communicates a universal and inclusive message with no social divides or segmentation.

Jack Daniel's brand image stayed consistent through time (same campaign since 1954), countries, and channels, making it all the more recognizable, distinctive and relevant.

The brand architecture is not based on aging, like other whiskies. Gentleman Jack targets older people with a bit more gravitas but remains unsophisticated and accessible. Single Barrel is the more sophisticated and trendier of the core range, which speaks to hipsters and works for food pairing. JD Tennessee Honey tries to create a bit of a different personality from its mother brand. It is more seasonal and fun, while the other flavor in the range, Tennessee Fire, created in response to the phenomenal success of Fireball, is more tactical.

Their digital strategy consists of one core website, jackdaniels. com, where all the sub-brands live. Their presence on social media (Facebook, Twitter, Instagram, YouTube) is the most powerful of all the mainstream spirit brands.

On social media, Jack Daniels utilizes four essential themes of conversation, which are consistent from one country to another (unlike any other brand, there is no real localization of content, only local adaptation of the four themes):

– Rock music (always at the heart of communication, a source of content, and a call for events)
– Family and friends
– Traditional American food – barbecues, burgers and ribs
– Hard work & the American dream - blue-collar, self-made rural Americana

Their influencer strategy is focused on young people that represent American values: freedom, independence, rebellion, macho, rock&roll, and Harley Davidson to name a few. They have one important event per year: *Jack's birthday*. Since nobody knows when exactly he was born, his birthday is celebrated in September, conveniently situated just after the summer vacation (a low season for whisky) and before the important Christmas season.

By maintaining consistent, clear brand values, with a compelling story, and by finding a balance between recruitment and retention strategies, continuing to build relevance through pop culture, and maintaining an honest tone of voice (*Tell, Don't sell*), Jack Daniels has managed to create one of the most powerful brand personalities in the world.

Marketing in a digital world – a perspective

In his 1964 book, *Understanding Media: The Extensions of Man*, a pioneering study in media theory, Marshall McLuhan famously said: "the medium is the message". While he was rightly criticized for his reductionist approach, bringing together channels, codes, and messages under the overarching term of the *medium*, he was the first one to recognize that each new form of media shapes messages differently and engages the viewer in different ways.

Many brands have become worldwide phenomenon overnight through the strategic and aggressive use of social media. These networks are particularly effective for direct-to-consumer brands, especially as consumers increasingly rely on images and influencers for their purchasing decisions as opposed to touching and feeling the product themselves in-store. Digital marketing is here to stay, at least for some industries and some marketers, so it's important to study its use.

In 2020, social networks have developed negative reputations for failing to address issues such as fake news and disinformation, hate speech, fake viewership, feed manipulation, data theft and/or misappropriation, online bullying, and addictive behavior. A recent Forrester survey found out that 37% of American adults believe social media does more harm than good, and only 14% believe the information they read on social media is trustworthy.

In my opinion, all social advertisers that continue to use digital networks without asking for consumer safeguards misuse the networks and contribute to the noise and the clutter. That is why I believe that brands should only be active in social media if they have an authentic strategy that fits with the overall brand strategy and principles that benefits the consumer.

Many young or legacy brands create social media accounts and are shocked when they do not achieve the following or *trendiness* of their competitors. They are posting regularly, piling on the hashtags, and investing in expensive digital consultants. Why isn't it working? Furthermore, countless executives have complained to me that digital marketers are no better than their other marketing counterparts, in that despite the emphasis on metrics and reporting in the digital industry, brand heads generally have a lack of understanding as to what all these metrics mean. Digital marketing is still a relatively new phenomenon, so we're all learning as we go, but marketing directors that have been in the business for 10 to 20 years can be at a disadvantage due to their lack of experience and understanding in regards to digital analytics. This is not to say that these things cannot be learned. Quite the contrary - you do not need to be a digital marketing expert to understand how it works, ask thought-provoking questions, and make effective digital marketing decisions.

Why your digital marketing strategy isn't working

Brands across the globe are struggling to connect with digital consumers, particularly on social media. It's becoming more and more challenging to grab the scroller's attention, especially as the average consumer learns to recognize and distrust ads, quickly skipping to the organic content on their timeline. Let's break down the most common social media mistakes you're probably making and discuss some strategies to optimize your performance.

Find Your Channel

Every brand marketer has learned the importance of social media marketing, so they instinctively want to create a profile on every network available in order to reach as many potential consumers as possible. It's interesting that so many marketers take this approach despite the fact that no self-respecting marketing professional would flood all media channels (TV, print, etc.) with the same messaging expecting a positive result. Ask yourself the following questions:

1. What channels are your target customers active on?
2. What channels are your competitors active on and what is their strategy?
3. What type of messaging do you want to promote and how does it fit with the channel's personality?

As we saw in the *Effective frequency* chapter, you need to balance reach with frequency to maximize effective reach, and depending on your budget, you might need to choose one or two digital channels to focus on only in order to achieve that.

Understand your customers' social media behaviors

You need to understand the different channels and their respective demographic characteristics to determine which ones fit within your overall brand strategy. If you are still not sure, analyze your competitors closely to understand which channels they see the most success on and try to figure out why. What kind of content do they post and what kind of engagement do they see? There are plenty of competitor analysis tools you can use to keep an eye on the competition.

Tailor your messaging to the channel

Just like a marketer would tailor an advertising campaign to a specific country or region, you want to tailor your content strategy to each social media network. Instagram posts perform best when they include high-quality photo and video content, with witty captions and an opportunity for followers to interact with the brand or with each other. If you are not prepared to create these types of posts, don't waste your energy on this network.

Furthermore, just because you are looking to leverage social media as a marketing tool doesn't mean you should be promoting product photos and other sales material exclusively on your social media accounts. To keep your followers engaged, post a mix of promotional material, lifestyle posts, and other media to capture their attention. Your audience will appreciate unique campaigns and content that set you apart from the competition, whether it's taking them behind the scenes, running a giveaway, or starting a viral trend they can participate in with their friends.

Track success

The number one complaint I hear from marketing directors, particularly in the spirits industry, where digital marketing remains a relatively small percentage of the overall marketing budget, is that social media marketing is opaque and difficult to report on. You are running a bunch of ads, and you know they're being seen around the world, but what is the tangible impact on sales?

The answer to this question is tracking. Conversion tracking has become increasingly sophisticated precisely in order to allow brand owners and managers to understand the true power of social media in terms of sales. The answer, on channels such as Instagram and Facebook, are pixels, which are placed throughout your website for conversion tracking purposes. The pixel follows your prospect not only as he or she browses your website, but also after they leave, to allow for remarketing. Create conversion events on your website to be able to accurately track the results of your social media campaigns.

Test, report, repeat

Many brands put a lot of time and effort into standing up their paid digital campaigns up and running, but often view it as a *set it and forget it*. Once the campaigns are live, surprisingly few companies task a specific marketing professional with reporting on performance.

The basic success metrics your company should measure on a consistent basis are conversions, and costs per clicks and conversion, as these metrics best demonstrate return on investment. However, it is important not to fall into the trap of focusing too much on cosmetic metrics such as impressions that often don't have a long-lasting impact on your brand awareness, or pivoting campaign strategy based on daily fluctuations. As a best practice, networks recommend not making any changes to your campaigns in the first two weeks.

Talk to your audience

If you truly build your social media following and connect with your client base, you are going to have to do more than just dump money into digital advertisements and post on a consistent basis. There are many ways to engage with your audience: responding to comments, following back, re-posting followers' content, hosting giveaways, and so on. Not only do these types of activities help to engage your followers, but it helps with the algorithms. Instagram, Facebook, and YouTube use engagement as a key metric to prioritize content on people's feeds.

Try influencer marketing

Influencer marketing is the millennial spin on the age-old practice of celebrity promotion, and brands across the world have enjoyed tremendous success as a result of their partnerships with prominent online personalities. Influencers have a unique ability to influence their followers' purchasing decisions through the relationships they have built through their social media channels, be it Instagram, YouTube, or TikTok.

In 2018, a majority of brands engaged in some type of influencer marketing campaign in the US, and this number is only expected to grow as an increasing number of consumers make purchasing decisions while scrolling through their social media feeds. But don't be fooled. Influencer marketing is not as easy as it seems, and it is not a sure-fire success. The key is to partner with the right influencers for your brand and to pursue collaborations that make sense for all parties involved.

How do you identify the influencers you want to work with and ensure that they provide a tangible value for your business? First, narrow your search to influencers that directly align with your target audience. You want the partnership to be authentic and believable, or else your potential customers simply will not buy it. While follower count is clearly important, it is also critical to look beyond that number and pay attention to the engagement on their posts. Smaller influencers often have higher engagement rates and a more personal relationship with their audience, which can translate into a higher conversion rate. Influencer marketing is another digital marketing domain that is extremely susceptible to fraud. Buying a following is now commonplace, and brands are being duped on a daily basis into signing expensive agreements with influencers that are only being followed by bots.

Once you have picked the right influencer, make sure the partnership aligns with your budget, desired outcome, and legal regulations. Your contract must respect the FTC Guidelines for Endorsements and Disclosure which requires the influencer to disclose that the partnership is paid. In terms of pricing, influencers have different rates depending on the platform and following. Most influencers are open to flexible payment agreements and performance-based contracts, especially if they are confident in their ability to actually influence their followers' purchasing behaviors. But make sure you have a way to track return on investment for your engagement. This is a major sore spot for brands because they don't know how to accurately measure the influence of their influencers. Affiliate codes are generally the easiest and fastest way to attribute sales directly to influencers.

The type of engagement you embark upon with your chosen social media star should depend on the business objective you have set for the campaign in question. If you are looking to maximize brand awareness, work with multiple influencers with different types of followers. If you are looking to capitalize as much as possible on your chosen influencer's following, many brands collaborate with influencers to create brand new products or spin-offs as part of their product line. This type of collaboration tends to be successful, as followers often want to support their favorite influencers by buying their products. Return on investment is easy to calculate because you can directly attribute all sales at least in part to the influencer.

However, influencer marketing should not dominate your social media strategy. If your Instagram feed begins to look like a series of business deals, your followers and customers will almost certainly be put off. Your brand needs to be authentic. To achieve this, your social media pages should have balanced content and your influencer collaborations should make sense for your brand.

Experiment with new digital marketing strategies and techniques

Is your marketing team really taking the time to test new digital marketing strategies to keep up with ever-changing trends? Here are a few tools that have been shown to lead to higher conversion rates and are often under-utilized by digital marketers.

Shoppable Ads

Have you ever seen a product on Instagram and loved it so much you wished you could purchase it directly, without having to navigate to the company/s website and dig through its product page? Well, it turns out you can, if the company is doing a good job of using the social media features available to them. Instagram allows brands to tag products within their organic content to enable a faster checkout process. When shoppers click *learn more*, they are immediately brought to an in-app product details page where they can check out without closing their app. You can also use the *swipe up* feature on Instagram stories to direct users to the product page on your website and remove friction in their shopping process. Based on the early success of these shoppable ads, Instagram is now in the process of rolling out *checkout on Instagram,* which will make browsing even easier by allowing users to complete in-app checkouts.

Chatbots

New developments in artificial intelligence have allowed sales conversations to be digitized to increase conversions and lower costs. How? Chatbots are software applications designed to simulate human conversations through rule-based scripts that help shoppers through their journeys. Chatbots provide immediate customer support and, depending on how advanced the technology is, can also provide personalized recommendations and offer discounts when it appears your company is about to lose a sale. Throughout the conversation, chatbots collect valuable information about the user that can later be used to analyze macro trends and inform your overall marketing strategy.

Establish clear creative governance

We know from experience that overperforming brands maintain consistency in their creative assets, as it increases brand recognition and salience and improves effectiveness over time. Chasing the latest fad from superficial social audiences could damage the effectiveness of the brand as consumers struggle to understand what the brand stands for. Marketers can control for this by establishing clear governance on how they adapt the creative to be relevant to the targeted audience and show a new side to the brand without confusing consumers.[71] For big brands, this can be achieved by using sharing platforms and consistent assets tagging. Marketers can further reduce the risk by applying this branding strategy consistently through aligned targeting and maintaining it for longer periods of time. [69]

SEVEN
Marketing organization

As we celebrated the history of advertising in Chapter 1, it's only fair to also celebrate those marketers that had a big influence on how marketing organizations are structured. In 1931, when Procter & Gamble had a one-page memo rule, Neil McElroy, as a junior executive managing the advertising campaign for P&G's Camay soap, wrote a three-pager that led to P&G's legendary brand-manager system. He later put the company into radio's daytime soap opera schedules and had P&G produce soaps for daytime TV. McElroy was P&G's executive committee chairman at the time of his death.[51] Since the 1960s, the most common job titles within advertisers are brand managers, product managers, marketing managers and marketing directors.

The P&G system was based around the brand or product manager and was focused on the product rather than on customers, users, or prospects. The product manager interacts with various other functions, including manufacturing and distribution, R&D, legal, accounting, market research, sales, purchasing, packaging, media and advertising, but there was no customer in sight. All contacts were internal. [51] The brand manager organization is based on an industrial-age organization in fact, which was built on concepts borrowed from the manufacturing industry. Traditionally structured firms are highly hierarchical, with the various functions (finance, marketing, sales, operations, IT, HR) designed to report upwards through the ranks to top management so that the task of senior managers is simplified to controlling functional heads.

There is very little literature on how to structure and refine your marketing organization. Most multinational companies rely on a traditional structure, very similar to P&G's original organization, no matter the industry. On the other hand, start-ups might not even have a formal marketing function inside the organization, equating marketing with sales. We are all familiar with the saying that, at a start-up, one must wear many hats.

Marketing functions and organization take different forms, depending on:

- size of the business
- size of A&P budget
- the strategic importance of the market
- salary levels in the respective market
- structure of the business (ex: sales by channels, in particular size of e-commerce within the overall turnover)
- competitive benchmarks
- the complexity of the business (ex: % of media in overall A&P budget)
- level and sophistication of the competition

When conflict appears in the overall organization, or when results are not up to management expectations and a restructuring needs to take place, there are no clear guidelines on how to tackle this transformation.

During my consultancy assignments, I was tasked with reorganizing marketing organizations across different geographies, and I have developed five takeaways that can guide your efforts in reorganizing your marketing department:

1: Create a marketing team mission that aligns with the overall company strategy

Marketing team members often complain that they are extremely busy with internal projects, reports, and meetings and do not have enough time to think about the big picture. If you ask each individual member what they think their priority should be, you will rarely find alignment.

But the alignment of your marketing team around key priorities is a must if you want to deliver remarkable results. Therefore you need to create a marketing team mission that represents a win-win between management expectations (financials, like profitable growth, market share gains, margins) and customer needs (be they retailers, wholesalers, shoppers, consumers, or internal customers like the wider marketing community). The mission should be clear both in terms of what the team is working to achieve and how the objective is best achieved (working together as a team, openly discussing difficult issues, etc).

To begin, you can start by aligning the CEO's priorities with customers priorities, as identified by the marketing team. Then refocus the team on the big issues, i.e. the issues that are both company priorities and a customer need.

Fine-tune your team mission around seven main pillars:

- Improve brand focus by having a balanced allocation of brands and their respective A&P across roles (A&P per headcount and department)
- Better balance between long term brand building and short-term activation
- Audit the agency partners: number of agencies used per type of activity, quality of interaction, value-added, budget allocation per agency
- Find out how your company compares to other players in the industry (usually achieved by interviewing agencies and key customers)
- Find out what you should reduce or eliminate at a team level (activities that suck up time but add little value)
- Free up time for KPI setting and project/activity evaluation
- Achieve cross-functional cooperation between marketing, user experience, product development, and finance to address powerful behavioral biases introduced by the advance of online

2: Design the right skills mix

Building a well-aligned team with the right marketing and leadership skills is critical for the success of your marketing department and your company. The recent focus on digital and data skills as a result of the recent spike in paid digital marketing has meant that other marketing experience and skills have become neglected. As we discussed in previous chapters, aligning with the company's overall strategy, understanding customer needs, understanding how advertising works, developing engaging communications that fit the brand objectives, and finding the right combination between touchpoints are still at the heart of a winning marketing strategy.

Getting great new people to work for you is challenging but very rewarding. Working with the best is not only a budget question, it is a returns question. If you succeed, you will get either a good financial return and/or an improved position in the market.

As marketing becomes more analytical and complex, it raises both technical and organizational challenges. You need to decide what to internalize and what to externalize. Choose the best external partners to work with, decide which skills are the must-haves within the organization and need to be learned, and which activities are better outsourced to agencies that can provide a high quality of work without the hassle of onboarding and training.

According to Thomas Barta and Patrick Barwise [44], getting the right mix between team skills and alignment is the single biggest driver of senior marketers' business impact. But while seventy-six percent of senior marketers are confident their teams are Masters of Marketing strategy, there is a significant mismatch between the skills that matter and the skills marketers have, especially in those more analytical areas, like pricing or data management. Meanwhile, social and digital media skills are not considered critical for business success and can be easily outsourced. Of course, this can differ by industry, market maturity, and legal constraints; that is why you need to create your own list of skills for what you are trying to achieve.

When building a team, clarity in the job description in regard to which competencies are really relevant for the business is super important. Focus on these distinctive skills that your team must truly excel at, and group them into two categories: analytic and creative. Look also at the personality traits you are looking to attract. Do you need more entrepreneurial people or more creative people? Do you need people with good internal and external networks? Which characteristics/personalities do not fit into your organization? Is your team diverse enough in terms of thinking, experience, and background? Which skills do you need to develop internally, and which skills do you need to buy?

As we mentioned in the Phronesis marketing chapter, establishing a structural marketing skills training path during the marketer's first years at the company is a must. Basic functional marketing skills (that can be developed internally), basic marketing leadership skills (that can be tailored to the skills needed) and required functional on-the-job experience are a must-have in a Training and Development Program.

Every company can and should carefully plan enhancements in the organization of the marketing department. These improvements will help you serve customers better now and build stronger and better brands in the future. They will force you to keep up with the market developments and improve both your top line and your bottom line while improving overall organizational efficiency.

3: Solving the sales & marketing conflict

The main conflict to solve, most often, is between the Sales and Marketing departments, which both undervalue the contribution of the other. When sales are bad, marketing blames the salesforce for poor execution of an otherwise excellent marketing plan and accuses them of being too focused on short term results. On the other hand, the sales team claims that marketing is disconnected from reality and therefore rolls out campaigns that do not sell, with a wrong touchpoint mix focused too much on the long-term, while setting unrealistically high prices for the brands that are not supported by a strong brand equity. Sales teams tend to claim that they could use some of the marketing budget to run sales promotions and incentives that will bring in more sales.

There are two underlying reasons for the conflict: budget allocation and personality.

The fight over budget allocation starts from top management. Usually, CEOs see sales as more contributive to the bottom line than marketing, unless the CEO has a marketing background, which is quite rare nowadays. The fight over budget is mostly a political fight (who has more power in the organization). In the political fight, marketing expenses have higher visibility, while sales expenses are mostly hidden in Allowances and Discounts, which are often off-invoice and therefore more difficult to quantify on a monthly or quarterly report (some costs are annual, for example, like retroactive discounts). On the other hand, sales have the final say on transactional price, even if marketing is supposed to be responsible for setting recommended retail prices.

The personality fight is due to the two different types of personalities that the two functions attract. Marketers are generally more highly educated, more creative, and project focused. Their job responsibilities typically revolve around medium- and long-term objectives, and therefore marketing employees are more difficult to judge based on short term performance. Salespeople are savvier about their customers, better negotiators, skilled relationship builders, used to adversity and rejection, and therefore easier to be judged on short term performance.

If this conflict is occurring within your organization, you can:

-   Focus on clarifying their tasks (using RACI for example), including clear rules of engagement, thresholds, and hand-off points for important tasks

- Have regular common meetings and seminars/conferences to improve communication and prevent disputes
- Align incentives and share systems to understand each other's performance metrics and rewards system
- Work against common team targets, rather than separate or individual targets
- Reward collaboration by having shared metrics and clarify expectations
- Create joint assignments and rotate jobs

4: Solving internal marketing department conflicts

Tensions can also exist within the marketing department. I know from experience that marketers often find it hard to deal with tense team dynamics and are generally less effective at managing conflict in a way that strengthens the team. Marketers are renowned for having inflated egos and are usually the most unhappy department in the organization (maybe because they also have the highest expectations).

Good conflict management is essential for building a cohesive and productive team, and is usually centered around five main pillars:

- Clarify roles & responsibilities within the department
- Align roles and responsibilities with the job description
- Reduce roles and responsibility overlap
- Clarify career path within the organization
- Detect sources of lack of trust and confidence that deteriorate team culture

In many organizations, marketers hide problems from their bosses because they do not want to show weakness. As a result, bosses underestimate the extent to which problems exist in the organization. Building an atmosphere of trust takes time, but it is worth it: teams that reach a high level of openness and collaboration are the most productive.

Despite your best efforts, usually because of personality conflict or political fight over budgets, sometimes interpersonal conflicts occur, and if you do not address them, they will only get worse over time. I would recommend tackling them as soon as possible through in-person discussions to find the source of conflict and work towards a resolution by bringing your HR expert.

5: Use existing best practices to evaluate the size and structure of the team

The quality of the people in your organization makes the difference, no matter the size of the budget and the competitive pressure. Once you have identified the gap between your actual marketing capabilities and the ideal set of skills you believe you need to succeed, define training programs to close the gap and benchmark against similar organizations in other geographies if you are an international company, or with your competitors in the same market, no matter the size of your company. LinkedIn can be of great help in this respect.

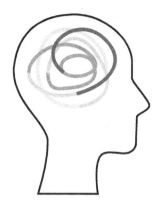

EIGHT

How small brands can fight big brands. The craft spirits case

In our ever-changing world, categories are constantly being restructured, innovation is constantly changing the rules of the game, and competition is growing exponentially no matter the industry. New segments can appear that open the doors to smaller brands because consolidation and fragmentation continue to co-exist.

Large companies might have a very different agenda when it comes to marketing than start-ups or small companies do. The marketing priorities of a large company are in response to the expectations of the board of directors (growing profit year after year). Small companies just want to make a profit, even if it is lower than last year's, as long as they can add value to the business.

If you want to beat the big guys at their game you need to have an entrepreneurial mindset: entrepreneurs are successful precisely because they are more innovative and creative, as they are not constrained to doing only those things that make sense to a Board. As Rory Sutherland says: "Interestingly, the likes of Steve Jobs, James Dyson, Elon Musk, and Peter Thiel often seem certifiably bonkers; Henry Ford famously despised accountants–the Ford Motor Company was never audited while he had control of it. When you demand logic, you pay a hidden price: you destroy magic. And the modern world, oversupplied as it is with economists, technocrats, managers, analysts, spreadsheet-tweakers and algorithm designers, is becoming a more and more difficult place to practice magic–or even to experiment with it" [27]. But being *illogical* does not mean to be disorganized or to not have a vision and a strategy.

To paraphrase Adam Morgan [44], marketing is not a science but rather an informed judgment. Creativity can have a more profound impact on business success than all the board expertise in the world. Innocent was started by people with no experience in smoothies. Austrian entrepreneur Dietrich Mateschitz had experience in marketing detergents and toothpaste when he launched Red Bull. Bert Beveridge had a career in the oil and gas industry and a stint in the mortgage trade when he started Tito's Vodka in the 90s, now worth an estimated 2.5 B$.

Entrepreneurs are facing the fundamental dilemma of how to make their businesses work with scarce resources when they have limited options to build revenue streams. It is not the same marketing strategy when you are dealing with 10 Million $ or 10 thousand $. You can achieve a lot with a very low advertising budget (much lower than your competition) through innovative, smart PR initiatives and stunts, the charismatic personalities of your leader(s), or a combination of these.

Apart from creativity and innovation, entrepreneurs need to differentiate themselves as being small, local, artisanal producers that are more connected to their communities, as well as more "human" and authentic than their much bigger corporate competitors. This has been the essence of the craft movement, whether it's beer, spirits, or soft drinks, that redefined the fundamental way we think about and interact with long-established categories.

In this chapter, we will analyze the craft spirits case and see the elements that make entrepreneurs successful in this area.

a. Why there is a need for small challenger brands

The importance of creating new (sub)categories

Markets for many product categories are mature and saturated. Any real growth comes from population increases, which never exceeds 1 or 2% every year, and from consumer trends that switch from one category to another (for example, the latest gin craze came mainly at the expense of the premium vodka category). To survive, a new product must steal market share away from other, established brands, or create a new (sub)category, or both. Red Bull and Puerto de Indias strawberry gin, for example, accomplished both.

Big brands are becoming commodities

In the 2000s, many brands are in decline because there has been an industry shift away from brand-building advertising to promotional programs and short-term advertising; from communication that conveys a distinctive positioning strategy to communications that focus on brand essence or imagery; from information-oriented to entertainment-oriented advertising. A large part of growth comes from category growth rather than from consumer brand switching. As a result, many brands are becoming commodities in consumers' minds. Consumers perceive the leading brands as becoming increasingly similar, meaning a low price becomes more important than a brand name. That is why your brand needs to bring something **fresh, distinctive** to the market in order to succeed.

The problems with line extensions

Big brands innovate through brand extensions. Many marketing executives believe that line extensions are less risky than launching new products. Or they believe that, because line extensions are easier to develop and introduce than completely new brands, they are more profitable. Sometimes, a cost accounting illusion creates this impression: when reporting costs for a brand extension launch, some costs are allocated to the mother brand instead of the brand extension, thus distorting the true profitability picture.

For example, in the spirits industry, most innovations come from flavor extensions (ex: strawberry pink gin, elderflower vodka, cinnamon whisky). This is what Sergio Zyman, the former CMO of Coca Cola once called *lazy marketing* - the idea that when the going gets tough for your core brands and it seems too hard to grow, you are better off filling the channel with line extensions and niche products. But this is not always the case: brand extensions can be riskier to launch than a new brand, because they might cannibalize the mother brand at a lower profitability rate, and in some cases might affect the brand or even the category in the long term (ex: the flavored vodka category in the US is credited for the decline of the category as a whole). Or think about the Vanilla Coke flop.

Retailers tend to give more space to new brands as a proportion of sales than to established brands

Suppose leading Brand X has a 40% market share in Category Y, and a typical retailer offers 50 faces for that category on his shelves. It is extremely rare that the retailer will offer 20 facings (40% of 50) for a single brand, even if it has different brand extensions. On the contrary, a new brand will typically get 1 face, which is the equivalent of a 2% share, even if it starts from scratch.

The anti-globalization and anti-industrialization movement

Some craft companies like Oxford Artisan Distillery are grain-to-glass craft distilleries using heritage grain located in their area. They use this in their marketing messaging to tap into the small but lucrative market for handmade, locally produced drinks. This is a market that the spirits giants struggle to cater to, although big brands like Absolut Vodka source their raw ingredients in an area close to the distillery in Sweden, while many craft gins can be quite opaque, being made under contract rather than in a specific area. It is a similar story with whisky: often the whisky from an island distillery will be stored in a giant warehouse near Glasgow rather than soaking up the seaside air.

b. The craft spirits case

Following the success of craft beer over the past few decades in the United States, the spirits industry started to catch up with the craft movement. Indeed, there is a general shift happening in consumer preferences, away from mass-produced brands and towards spirits made through craftsmanship, although not at the same pace as in the beer industry and not in all spirits categories. This trend is driven by consumer trends: an anti-globalization movement and the search for identity and authenticity, and it is here to stay. The coronavirus might amplify this trend once the crisis is behind us.

We will have a few years intermezzo due to the coronavirus crisis; however, this is not due to fundamentals, but rather to financing issues that entrepreneurs might face in case of unexpected events, like the one we experience as I write this book, the COVID-19 crisis and the impact of the lockdown on the on-trade industry. According to trade associations, the European Union's 25% tariff on American whiskey and the US's tariff on single malt Scotch have hit small producers the hardest. It is therefore even more important than before to build a sustainable business model and strong brands in order to survive against mega companies which have a bigger portfolio diversity and strong financials, and therefore can better cope with margin and cash flow pressure. For the producers that manage to survive through COVID-19, their uncertainties are likely to continue in the medium and long-term, as the global economic recession will likely reduce the consumers' willingness to purchase super premium brands, as witnessed during the last recession. Shoppers' proven predilection for familiar, trusted products in times of crisis means the companies with strong brand recognition will fare best. Furthermore, since the in-person marketing channel is and will continue to be hit the hardest by the pandemic, and since bartenders play an essential role in promoting craft brands through interactions with their customers, it will be even harder for these craft brands to recruit new consumers.

Micro distilling (also known as craft distilling or artisan distilling) is what people call smaller distillers (usually producing less than 100,000 cases per year). The term differentiates between large, multinational brands (producing tens or hundreds of millions of cases per year) and the craft producers, in much the same way that microbrewers were separated from larger breweries twenty years ago. While it is true that the growth of the micro distilling industry matches the growth of the microbrewing industry, there are some key differences between them. According to Just Drinks, there are now more than 2,000 craft distilleries operating in the US, and sales have consistently outpaced the total spirits market, up 25.5% by volume and 27% by value in 2018 according to the ACSA. The IWSR, meanwhile, has claimed there are decades to go until the sector reaches saturation point and starts to backpedal. [42]

Most large breweries make more or less the same style of beer, with similar taste due to process automation and similarity of ingredients used, while craft brewers appeared to satisfy the needs of a large segment of beer consumers that was looking for something different. In the world of distilled spirits, on the other hand, consumers can find a large selection of many different high-quality spirits at any liquor store. By focusing on utilizing the unique ingredients and flavors of their region of provenance, a resource that few other large distilleries have access to, the micro distillers can create a competitive advantage.

There are also some key similarities between the microbrewing and micro distilling movements, as well as with the successful mega brands that managed to adapt their marketing to the increased desire for authenticity and storytelling. Their tasting rooms and shops located at the distillery are open for tours, tastings, and shopping (including unique merchandise, products, like personalized bottles, and experiences, not available anywhere else), being a local attraction and promoted by the local tourist agencies. Customers who enjoy the experience of learning about the craft of distilling and blending are welcome to visit, taste the products where they are produced and get their spirits and information direct from the source, while buying a few bottles (including some *distillery specials*) for home enjoyment.

Successful micro distillers are also committed to the quality of their products, the authenticity of their ingredients, and the innovative processes and recipes used. Global consumers associate *craft* with high-quality ingredients that are handmade and authentic. Craft/ artisanal claims and production are a way to premiumize spirits offerings, but just 15% of spirits drinkers say that craft/artisanal production would encourage them to pay more; therefore, there is an opportunity to associate and combine this approach with other premiumization factors, including unique or better taste, food pairing, and even natural ingredients to enhance the premium nature of the product offering and justify a higher price point.

Questions:

1. Contact a local tourist agency. What are the local attractions, stories, legends, landmarks that delight tourists in your area that could be a base for your brand story?

2. What personal story do you have linked to spirits (like your grandfather being a merchant selling spirits in a local shop, an old spirits recipe found in the attic, etc.)? Do you have any old photos and documents that can be used to build a story? Check your heritage tree: can you find some interesting facts that could build a story?

3. Contact a local institution that deals with agricultural products or local farmers: what are the local premium agricultural ingredients specific to your region?

c. The gin and whisky case

Not so many years ago, the gin category was in decline and four big brands from the biggest spirits manufacturers (Gordon's and Tanqueray from Diageo, Beefeater from Pernod Ricard and Bombay

Sapphire from Bacardi) were dominating the category. Nowadays, when ordering a gin & tonic, rather than being offered a choice between Gordon's or Beefeater (or no choice at all), you might be handed a menu filled with 20 brands' tasting notes and widely different price ranges. There might even be recommendations for which tonic water to have with your gin: from redesigned premium Schweppes (that comes in a smaller bottle) to Fever Tree to Fentimans, to mention just a few.

There has been an explosion in new distilleries over the last 10 years – the most noticeable are the gins, but there are also new whiskies (Irish whiskeys distilleries, in particular), vodkas, and rums appearing on the market every year.

Tens of distilleries are opening every year in every country. What happened?

Some of this is explained by regulation: in the UK the first small scale (lower than 1,800 liters) distilling license for nearly 200 years was granted in 2009. You can now obtain a license to make gin in your bar as long as you can show that you have a viable business plan. Since in England it was quite common for people living in the countryside to make sloe gin by macerating sloe berries in gin, these licenses created an immediate supply. The same phenomenon occurred in other countries throughout Europe.

On the other hand, the cost of entry is pretty low (if you do not need to age your product), like in the case of vodka and gin. By EU law, to make your gin you have to use 96% neutral grain alcohol, which most craft producers buy at a very affordable price (there is an overcapacity of production in the EU), because you need a very tall and expensive industrial still to make very pure alcohol. The base spirit can then be turned into gin by diluting the alcohol with water, putting it in a small copper pot still (which can cost about few thousand dollars) with a basket above containing the botanicals, then heating it so that alcohol vapor passes through the basket, picking up your desired gin flavors, and then watering down to 40% alc. The investment ranges from 700K$ for a vodka or gin brand to 5M$ for a whisky brand. Many new whisky distillers also make a gin or a vodka to bring in some cash while the whisky matures in oak casks (min 3 years in the UK, but only one year in the US). But one of the learnings of Sidney Frank, that we met in the Jägermeister case study, still holds true today: you need a lot of money for bricks and mortar: *don't build a distillery until you have enough money to do it properly and enough production to put in it.*

The founders of craft spirit brands are usually either former executives from the spirits industry or corporate guys (mainly from the tech, finance, or insurance industries) looking for a new experience. For example, the inventor of Monkey 47 gin is an ex-Nokia executive.

According to Guardian [29], companies such as the Cotswolds Distillery and Shed 1 tap into the small but lucrative market for handmade, locally produced drinks, a market that the spirits giants struggle to cater to. Both Tanqueray and Gordon's London dry gins are made in Scotland (though craft gin can be equally opaque; many are made by Thames Distillers under contract rather than in a small village in a bucolic location). It is a similar story with whisky. Almost all those picturesque Highland distilleries are in the hands of multinational companies such as Diageo, headquartered in London, Pernod Ricard in Paris, or Suntory in Osaka. Often the whisky from an island distillery will be stored in a giant warehouse near Glasgow rather than soaking up the seaside air.

While Scotch whisky doesn't have to contain any Scottish barley, craft whiskies can offer a *grain to bottle* experience. Darren Rook at the London Distillery Company in Battersea even uses a particular strain of barley called plumage archer that almost died out after the first world war. The only place he could find it was on the Prince of Wales's estate in Cornwall. Alasdair Day, the co-founder of R&B Distillers, which has just started distilling on the Isle of Raasay near Skye, says he buys all the grain from Inverness, but is looking at growing hardy Swedish and Icelandic strains of barley varieties on Raasay itself [29].

The big producers will tell you that the variety of barley doesn't matter, that it is just about creating sugar to turn into alcohol. But some in the whisky world think that Scotch lost something when it became more efficient in the 70s and 80s. Sukhinder Singh from online retailer The Whisky Exchange laments the days when "everything was done by hand, cereal was more natural and fermentations went on for longer". Rook agrees, arguing that "Scotch has become very homogenized." When he worked at the Scotch Malt Whisky Society, he adds, he "tried old whiskies that the modern stuff can't compete with" [29].

Whisky is essentially distilled beer, so it is not surprising that many producers get into distilling via beer. David Vitale, the founder of Starward whisky in Melbourne, Australia, says that his team is split evenly between people who come from a beer background and those who come from wine. They play with different roasts of barley to make "an in-your-face Australian whisky", as he puts it. Going one step further, Corsair Distillery in Nashville, Tennessee, makes a hopped whiskey from IPA beer. Yeast is another area of experimentation. According to Rook, "they use an old strain from Whitbread brewery that gives a meaty character to the whisky, like older Macallan." Compare this with Diageo, which uses the same yeast in all of its whiskies. Unlike the big players, the small players don't need to be consistent; every batch can be different [29].

This very inconsistency gives smaller distillers a point of differentiation that can drive value and allow them to sell at a premium, especially to the connoisseurs. The micro distillers can focus on what goes into their whisky, rather than the old traditional clichés used to sell big brands of Scotch or Bourbon. As Rook puts it: "Scotch marketing is reliant on bagpipes, lochs, and glens when it should be about yeast, diversity, and barley." It is the same in the US. Corsair's whisky, founded in 2008 in Bowling Green, KY by Darek Bell and Andrew Webber. They have labels that remind consumers of Tarantino movies while Boondocks bourbon bottles look more like cognac. It is a different aesthetic world.

For all the excitement about craft distilling, it is still a drop in the ocean compared to the big brands. Glenfiddich, the market leader in the single malt whisky world, together with The Glenlivet, have recently extended their distilleries to produce an extra 13 million liters of pure alcohol a year. The Glenlivet, founded in 1824, the first licensed distillery in Scotland, sells in excess of 1 million cases per year. Meanwhile, the Cotswolds Distillery produces only about 11,000 cases liters a year. The four big brands in gin sell in excess of 18 million cases per year. The most successful craft gin brands sell about 100,000 cases.

That doesn't mean that the big producers are ignoring craft. Diageo has an investment arm, Distill Ventures, where small distillers can get money, expertise, and marketing clout. It is, according to Ian Buxton, the author of Whiskies Galore, "a cheap way for the bigger distillers to learn and experiment. It's nothing to them, a £250,000 investment — Diageo's Ewan Gunn is candid about what they get out of it: An insight into their (craft distilling) world. We get to know their business inside out and there is the opportunity to acquire successful brands in the future."

So, what does the future hold for all these new distilleries? As usual, a Darwinian story: some brands, such as Sipsmith, which was bought by Beam Suntory earlier last year, will get swallowed up by the big guys. Others will not be so lucky. There is a feeling in the industry that the gin market is saturated. With whisky, the worry is that the Scottish and Irish have doubled production in recent years and, by the time all the new whiskies are ready to drink, the global market will be in a downturn.

d. How to build a brand identity as a craft brand and thrive in a more difficult environment

To succeed and even to survive, you need to invest in developing your brand, as it is your major sustainable competitive advantage. In the beverage industry, 80% of the company value lies in intangibles, and the brand is a major part of it.

According to Thomas Barta and Patrick Barwise[44], to create a point of difference you might need to look at potential challenges of your target category:

- the fundamental driver of the category (what your brand rejects within the existing category)
- some aspect of the way the consumer shops for, experiences, or consumes your product
- the culture surrounding the category
- some broader aspect of contemporary culture

If you are a micro distiller, chances are that the geographic reach of your brands is pretty limited: nearly 50% of US craft spirits sales take place in distillers' home states, says the ACSA, with almost half of this home-state business taking place on-site at distilleries. Share of the total US spirits market, while growing, also remains relatively low for craft players, at 3.9% by volume and 5.8% by value. [42] This demonstrates that if the craft producers' focus remains on selling locally, they will not be able to survive against the big producers. On the other hand, if they turn their focus to the off-premise channel, where the power of big brands is more important than on-premise, their lack of experience, leverage, and supply chain expertise in this arena will be difficult to overcome. Therefore, a clever sales and marketing strategy is a must to survive.

To build a brand from scratch, you need to start with a simple plan. You might think that it is a waste of time to do it (I know from experience that entrepreneurs do not like brand plans), but the process you will go through is valuable in clarifying some of the key elements in your business. If you already have a brand, you can still check if you have all elements in order.

The one-page marketing plan

You can have a marketing plan like the big players but written on one page. I recommend you go through the process, as it will help you shape your business for years to come and you can come back to it to see where you were right and where you were wrong. Having a shortlist as described below to define, even as a draft, your brand, taking into consideration the competitive environment in which the brand will live, will increase the chances of success. Here is how you can do it:

Figure 24: One-page marketing plan

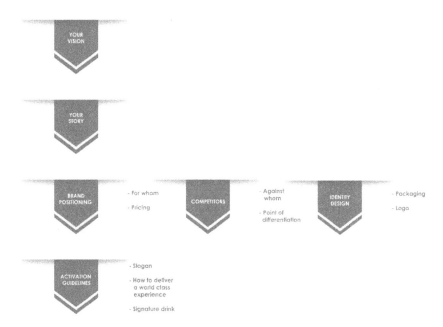

What is your vision of the business

What is the business opportunity: The category size in your target market(s), the structure of the market (main competitors in your target price segment, dynamics of the category and main actors, consumer trends, short analysis of main competitors, opportunity to enter the market). If you do not know the size of the market, you can check with your local producers' association. Assessing the size of the pie is crucial.

What is your ambition: What is your ambition in terms of sales over the next couple of years? Make sure you have a reasonable ambition (1% market share in 5 years might be a very ambitious target). Do you want to remain a local brand or expand beyond your state or country once you have the necessary resources?

How you will reach that ambition: Your financial investment needs, timeline, and basic P&L projection for 1-2 years.

Your story

Before you contact an agency to help you with the creative process, you need to develop a clear story that will guide the process. Big brands rely on lots of research, but entrepreneurs rely more on their gut feeling and market feedback.

To start your branding journey, you need to have a story. Not necessarily a USP, not a *Reason Why*, but a story. Your unique brand story answers the question of why your brand exists, why it is special, and why people should care. You need to be able to explain in a few words the meaning behind the product. *Usage pull* can measure this impact, and answers one question: *Does your story work?* Below is a more detailed list to inspire you to increase your brand pull:

- **Your brand name** should embody the big idea of your product, that is part of the brand story
- **History**: a long history of distilling in your area (ex: your area has a sandy beach, perfect for unloading banned liquor and making a dash back out to sea during Prohibition). Where did your brand come from?
- **Water/purity**: your area has crystalline spring water or deep clean water. Purity is often used as an attribute, especially for clear liquids like vodka.
- **Central figure of the founder**. Most successful micro distillers put their founders at the center of their story (ex: Tito's vodka)
- **Locally sourced and/or organic and/or rare/exotic ingredients**: using (at least some) locally sourced ingredients, with one *star*

ingredient, combined with soft spring water from local sources will be your secret weapon.

- **Distillation process**: your distillation process is unique due to your equipment, combination of traditional stills, distillation process, and technology. What sets you apart?
- **Maturation**: maturing your spirit in oak casks or maturing your concoction in earthenware containers give extra value to your spirit (unless your product category does not need maturation, like gin or vodka)
- **The production process**: any handmade process is a plus
- **Grain to glass** – the fact that you do everything on-site, including distillation for the base spirit, blending, aging, and bottling.
- **Family or partnership ownership** – the fact that the company is owned either by the family or a very small group of entrepreneurs /founders is often seen as authentic.

If you found a good story that resonates with your target, remember that being consistent and continuing to tell your story with a single-minded, uninterrupted campaign theme is critical. Frequent changes to your advertising campaigns will almost certainly negatively impact sales. When a campaign wears out, you will know it, but if you look at successful campaigns, they last even for 20-30 years.

Questions

1. Identify local bars in your area. Speak with the bartenders and bar managers: what are the trends? What kind of categories do they see blowing up? Test your story with them: what excites them, what doesn't? Do they like your bottle? If not, why not? Do they like your label? Can the

customers read the name of the brand? Do you have enough contrast with the label background?

Brand positioning

After your story is clarified, you can proceed with your brand positioning.

For whom: Think about your strategic target. These are usually consumers that are most likely to buy or promote your brand, because they identify with your brand promise. If you're just getting started, your strategic target may be the trendy bartenders living in your city and the surrounding area, as well as confident branded spirits drinkers, social, active, and creative types.

Against whom: Who are your main competitors, and therefore your main source of business, either from your category (ex: other craft gins, big international brands) or other categories (ex: craft vodkas)

Instead of a USP, use a **point of differentiation**, which is still considered by many fundamental to a successful branding strategy. It has to include attributes and benefits that consumers will strongly, uniquely, and positively associate with your brand, but most importantly why they should choose you instead of the competition. Below is an example:

- **Brand X** is [the world's only gin made in region Y using locally sourced pristine water and organic ingredients following a secret recipe and delivering a unique, superior taste]
- **Brand X** is [giving back to its community by sourcing local ingredients, creating jobs, and paying local taxes and having an environmentally friendly footprint production].

If you already have identified the **Brand values** and the **Brand personality** in your story, the emotional attributes associated with a specific brand will highlight why and how a brand does what it promises. If not, you can develop them later, after you receive feedback from the market.

Your price positioning: what will be your price index vs your main competitors

The competition

Remember, your competition might not be the big guys, but smaller players like yourself. Make sure your brand is not too similar to brands that are already out there.

Questions

- Can you identify your How, What, Where, When, and To Whom for your brand?
- Can you create a mood board for your brand? Use glossy magazines or search the internet to find ads for beverages and any other pictures that might inspire you. Cut them out, paste them on a big piece of paper or on your computer screen and group them by theme. Look for related words that express the emotion you are trying to capture.
- What are the distinctive design elements for your brand?
- Can you identify the top five values for your brand?

Brand identity

Brand identity is the most important element to make your brand distinctive so that buyers can easily, and without confusion, identify it. Branding and design are therefore a key part of marketing and a strategic element in everything you do. We explained above why your brand name should embody the big idea of your product. Your packaging design is the visual expression of that idea.

Given the increasing numbers of bottles and labels popping up on store shelves and bars across the globe, one of the biggest challenges when developing your brand strategy is design (bottle, label, colors, shapes, and symbols) and semiotics (typography, typefaces, and icons). However, these two elements will create a strong and unique identity that will cut through the 'shelf noise' and define your brand identity.

Packaging

Spirit lovers seem more likely than average consumers to spend time looking at the bottle and the label. According to Byron Sharp [56], spirits are perceived as the most differentiated category (almost double the average). As the craft spirits category becomes more competitive, good packaging design is not only an aesthetic pleasure, it is probably your most important asset. In some cases, it is the only communication vehicle that your brand has (especially in *dark* markets where you cannot advertise, or if you have a very limited budget). Remember, the packaging design has the biggest impact on consumers, especially if they are not already familiar with the brand. They usually think that, if the packaging is great, the product must be great as well.

You also need to take into consideration the needs of the bartenders: for example, they do not like bottles with either too large or too small necks that complicate the pour. The structural integrity of the glass is also important. Closures can be a problem too – for example, overly heavy wax dips.

Consider the needs of the retailers as well: bottles that are too tall or too top-heavy do not work well. Fat bottles that take up more than one slot on the shelf also cause problems with shelf space and might not be accepted.

The package design should include: the brand logo, the label shape, the neck label, the back label, the closure, the bottle shape, an icon or illustration, mandatories (product type, legal copy), and your descriptive copy.

The unique bottle shape is not only a visual cue; touch can induce a highly personal association with the product and a brand. Ideally the bottle should have a story by itself and be recognizable on the shelf.

A good design partner will help you bring your brand vision to life. Here is the list you need to think about when briefing your design agency:

Logo: Your logo is your brand's primary identifier, together with your proprietary bottle shape. Logos are usually composed of two elements: the brand typeface and the logo graphic. Logos can be of different types (pictorial, abstract, symbolic etc.)

Logo colors: you need to establish rules for brand messaging and packaging (ex: four/three-color version, two-color version, one-color version, B&W version).

Logo clear space: Always keep your logo clear of any graphics, imagery, or text. This protects the integrity of your logo and ensures it is seen as a unit and is never visually dominated by other elements.

Minimum reproduction sizes: Define the minimum size (ex: 22mm height for print or 93x115 pixels for on-screen applications)

Color palette: primary and alternate colors, when the core identity appears in series

Logo usage exceptions: ex: size for packaging closure, twice logos on shippers...

Typefaces: Fonts, typography, and so on

Pattern graphics: Graphic repeat patterns for use as surface treatment and for application for POS, publications, and presentations

Unacceptable core identity usage: The artwork must not be altered or used incorrectly or inappropriately, that is why you need to provide examples to demonstrate incorrect uses of core identity.

Questions:

1. Is your logo distinctive from your competitors, simple, and unforgettable? Is it recognizable from a distance?
2. Test your packaging with your local bartenders. Do they like your bottle? If not, why not? Do they like your label? Can the customers read the name of the brand? Do you have enough contrast with the label background?
3. Did you register your logo?
4. Did you ensure that your logo is developed and saved as a high-resolution image (min 300dpi)? This will ensure that the quality does not deteriorate when reproduced in large formats

Activation guidelines

If you plan to expand your sales territory, think about developing presentation materials, basic Point of Sale, and activation guidelines.

Even if you do not have a clear idea about your brand personality, it is important that you define your brand universe. Delivering a world-class experience for the brand, even with a limited budget, in a consistent way is critically important if you want to build a brand.

Slogan/taglines

Alongside the logo and the bottle, your slogan is also critically important to your overall brand. The slogan can be:

Descriptive: Helps to describe the product service or promise: *Red passion* (Campari), *Aperol Spritz* (Aperol), *It's not Scotch. It's not bourbon. It's Jack (Jack Daniels), Triple distilled, twice as smooth* (Jameson), *Start a party* (J&B whisky), *Vodka for dog people* (Tito's), *Schwarzwald Dry gin* (Monkey47), *No Martini, no party* (Martini), *Open your world* (Heineken), *The fun starts here* (Tuborg)

Superlative: Defines the product's market position: *Every pairing is perfect* (Smirnoff), *Absolut perfection* (Absolut vodka), *King of beers* (Budweiser), *Probably the best beer in the world* (Carlsberg), *You can't improve on the original* (Jim Beam)

Imperative: A command or a direction for action. Ex: *Keep walking!* (Johnnie Walker), *Live with Chivalry* (Chivas Regal), *Stay True* (Ballantine's)

Provocative: Using a provoking question or irony; Ex: *Got a little captain in you?* (Captain Morgan), *Un Ricard sinon rien* (Ricard), *Tomorrow is overrated* (Jose Cuervo)

The moderation line is also important for alcoholic beverages. Choose your own moderation line to ensure you are seen to be advertising responsibly in line with your brand identity (ex: *Your* *friends at Jack Daniels remind you to drink responsibly; Enjoy your Malibu moment responsibly* or simply *Drink responsibly*)

Signature drink/Drink strategy: appealing to the senses

A study on memory and the senses carried out at the Rockefeller University revealed that in the short term we remember just: 1% of what we touch, 2% of what we hear, 5% of what we see, 15% of what we taste and 35% of what we smell. [75] Smell and taste are the most sensitive of all our senses, that is why a lot of marketers in the spirits industry do tastings, using bartenders or more commonly brand ambassadors, or sampling in bars and free tastings in stores. Below you may find an example of drink strategy that is supposed to put your product in the best position when sampled to consumers.

Table 14: Example of drink strategy for a spirit brand

Core drinks	Consumer occasion	Usual place of consumption	Consumer target/ Objective
Tall&Short Cocktails; Indulgent	Signature drink, occasions	At home, in a style bar, in a casual bar, in a restaurant, in a nightclub, etc.	Strategic target vs consumption pool; Recruitment vs Retention

Brand architecture

Brand architecture is a way of describing the hierarchy of brands within the company's brand portfolio. You need to choose between:

o **A master brand** (or parent brand) with a number of separate, unique, trademarked brands

For example, Absolut Vodka is a master brand, while the flavor extensions have unique names but similar bottle shapes (Absolut

Peppar, Absolut Extrakt, Absolut Apeach, etc.) and the premium version (Absolut Elyx) has a different bottle shape and positioning. Similarly, Jack Daniels Old No7 is the mother brand, and Tennessee Honey and Tennessee Fire are flavor sub-brands with similar bottle shapes and labels, while Gentleman Jack and Single Barrel are premium expressions with different packaging and branding. Unlike other FMCG products (ex: L'Oreal, Nivea), it is very rare to see different spirits categories sit under one master brand (ex: Gordon's Gin and Gordon's vodka); when this happens, it is usually for standard brands

- o **A house of brands**, where each brand has a unique, distinctive personality. For example, Chivas Brothers has in its portfolio different Scotch whiskies brands, like Ballantine's, Chivas Regal, The Glenlivet, Longmorn, Aberlour, Scapa and Royal Salute

Your digital assets and the media budgets

The importance of digital assets in creating attractive content is a no-brainer for marketers. Engagement with marketing content increasingly occurs on websites and social platforms like Instagram and YouTube and mobile devices, turning online stories, images, and videos into crucial assets, especially as brands look to stand out and win consumers' attention. Unlike big brands, small brands are more reliant on direct sales through channels like Google Shopping or Shopify. It is likely that they will also have a high reliance on YouTube, Facebook, and Instagram to drive discovery and purchase.

You do not need to produce hundreds of assets to support your channels as big brands do. Production-rich content still has its place; think about both long-form video (for example, where you source your botanicals from) and short-form, that could be shared on your YouTube channel or your site. Nowadays, most marketers use engagement metrics such as clicks, likes, and shares as their key measure of success. While engagement metrics are important, hearing the voice of your current customers, as well as prospects, help in understanding the impact of your visual assets. Digital assets are also valuable to facilitate direct interaction with your prospective customers, by inviting them to visit your distillery, where you should convert them into regular customers.

Media is a significant investment and a key driver of business performance. Big brands tend to be media savvy. They have media directors or Chief Media Officers in-house whose task is to empower their marketing teams with best-in-class processes and support. And as a result, they fully know how to get the very best out of their media agency partnerships using media management best practices. They tend to get the best prices, the best people, the best media inventory, all in a very transparent way, and therefore getting their fair share of the cash rebates from their media agencies.

The challenge for small to medium advertisers is how to get the same benefits that the top global advertisers currently enjoy. You might think that having smaller media budgets will forbid you from getting similar deals. But this couldn't be further away from the truth. The correlation between media prices and size of media budgets no longer exist.

Increased complexity has enabled media agencies to create opaque financial structures and then inflate their fees and media prices at will, while many advertisers are stuck behind contracts unfit for modern media buying that provide little scope for transparency and accountability. Knowing media management best practices is what makes the difference between a best-in-class advertiser (with full transparency, competitive prices, and effective media planning) and an advertiser who relies too much on their media agency (and most likely gets the worse media inventory, at a premium price, without getting any or very little cash rebates).

The solution for small and medium advertisers, who can't afford hiring media directors in all key markets, is to educate and empower their marketing teams with the knowledge, skills and tools the big boys are using. For example, to help small and medium advertisers, Abintus, a small media consultancy start-up based in London, successfully created an online coaching platform (The Abintus Academy – *www.abintus.academy*) designed to teach them about media management best practices and improve their return on advertising spend. I had the pleasure to work with the co-founders of Abintus (Philippe Dominois & Tatjana Slykova) while CMO at Pernod Ricard EMEA&LATAM, and I was impressed with the depth of their media knowledge and their eagerness to innovate and create new media solutions to differentiate themselves from bigger media consultancies out there. If you are interested, you can get access to their platform with a special 30% discount using the following coupon code at checkout: (phronesismarketing).

Finding distributors

You will probably need to go with different distributors in different markets or states. Ideally go with small enough distributors who will give more share of mind to your product. When you decide to go to a new market, go visit the on-premise and retail accounts you want to be in and ask them who their favorite distributors are. Then go see them and make a great presentation to them. A distributor only puts as much effort into selling your brand as they see you putting in yourselves. Also, be aware that your distributor won't do anything for you if you don't do anything for them – you need to help them sell the product.

Consistently building your brand

Even if your brand has distinctive assets, they are not inherent. They need to be learned by the consumer until the links between them and the brand are learned and help create *memory structures*. To successfully do so, you need to be consistent over many years, even decades, not only in terms of message and positioning but also to the visual, verbal, and style of branding elements, across campaigns. Inconsistent communication and packaging changes can confuse the occasional buyers, so it is better to spend a lot of time to get it right the first time. Having distinctive assets will not motivate consumers to buy brands, but it helps them understand what the brand stands for, and will allow the development of loyalty. [56]

The case for craft spirits association

The COVID crisis has created a new incentive for micro distillers to team up: joint distribution agreements, joint marketing initiatives, coordination (like having one strategic planner coordinating their activities and organizing a common craft spirits fair), and joint purchases of raw materials are the most obvious opportunities.

Craft spirits producers can also join forces on content partnerships, like publications and web projects, although there may be a pride factor involved there that makes it very difficult to merge.

NINE

Meaning and purpose: social responsibility programs

Craft as well as socially responsible distillers take a long-term view on their impact on the environmental and architectural heritage of their local community. Some aim to become a zero-waste facility, have restored historic buildings, contribute to the development of local traditions and heritage, actively seek to leave a lighter carbon footprint, and invest in measures that boost biodiversity both at the distillery and in their raw material cultivation. Some distillers harvest rainwater, producing virtually no waste and employing a heat recovery system. For example, Slane distillery is focused on operating the distillery as sustainably as possible. "We use river water to cool our stills avoiding any refrigeration plant and equipment; our distiller's draff is used by a local dairy farmer to feed his cows; we recover waste heat from our Stillhouse and Brewhouse batches to heat up the next batches of brewing water and distillation washes coming through; we are treating our own effluent on-site and in the coming years as our production volumes grow, we will operate an Anaerobic Digester on-site generating natural gas to fuel one of our steam boilers. Working at one with nature is important for us here at Slane." [76]

Others are sourcing their ingredients locally, from the family farmland around the distillery, while improving soil health and boosting biodiversity.

Big companies are also responding to the socially responsible trends: Pernod Ricard announced it will achieve 100% water balanced in high-risk countries and 20% water-use reduction by 2030, 100% ban on single-use plastic POS and 100% renewable energy by 2025 and 50% reduction of overall intensity of carbon footprint in line with Science-Based Targets by 2030. During and after COVID, small and big distillers alike engaged in sustaining the bar community: for example, Diageo launched a $100 million global program recovery fund for bars. While small distilleries around the world helped produce and donated hundreds of tons of hand sanitizers.

In conclusion, companies are increasingly ramping up their focus on social responsibility, whether it is championing women's rights, protecting the environment, or attempting to reduce poverty, on local, national, or global levels. From a pure financial perspective, socially responsible companies project more attractive images to both consumers and shareholders, which in turn positively affect their bottom lines. It can also boost employee morale and lead to greater productivity in the workforce.

Questions:

What are you passionate about and will inspire you to get involved in your community?

What charity or local movement do you plan to support?

TEN
Conclusions

In an environment in which companies are under increased pressure to improve their turnover and profits ahead of the industry average, marketing remains the most important ingredient that determines company success and value creation. Unfortunately, for more than a decade, marketing, as an organizational function, has been downgraded from its strategic role to a marginalized tactical and sales support department. Marketing leaders must therefore demonstrate the business value of their efforts if they want to remain relevant to the C-suite.

Many companies have given up on finding the Holy Grail of marketing effectiveness, and more still are searching in vain to apply econometrics or artificial intelligence to a dataset that simply doesn't reflect the company's reality. Based on my experience, I have come to the conclusion that building a marketing effectiveness ecosystem, with a dedicated decision support system that is easy to understand and use, is adapted to industry/category specificities and that can be shared within the organization, and that is supported by relevant training, benchmarking and case studies, is the most important step in tackling effectiveness.

While recognizing that there are some general marketing laws that are useful to create a marketing epistemology, we are not trying to create a kind of general theory, but rather propose a broader, holistic view, in which we move beyond the purely analytical or technical to put to work and recognize the strengths of marketing as a social science using case studies as the base of Phronesis Marketing. Marketing is not a science but rather an informed judgment. Phronesis Marketing is about using your practical wisdom to make ever better-informed decisions and help improve the strategic position of the marketing profession within the company.

By supporting this framework with a Phronesis Marketing approach in terms of training and development of the marketing department, your chances of success in the marketplace can be maximized, even when your budgets are under pressure.

I hope that my book will help you better understand or remind you how advertising works in real life, and give you more confidence when deciding how to invest your money in order to achieve your strategic objectives and financial results. I also hope it will help you better structure your organizations in order to survive in this complex consumer environment.

I look forward to your feedback on how these ideas helped you achieve that. You can reach me at corneliu@effymarketing.com for any comments or questions, or message me on LinkedIn.

ELEVEN
Bibliography and references

(1) Feldwick, Paul - *The Anatomy of Humbug- How to think differently about advertising*, Matador, 2015

(2) Schumacher, E.F. - *Small is Beautiful*, Vintage, 1993

(3) Hopkins, Claude C. - *Scientific Advertising*, reprinted in 2015 by Amazon

(4) Batra, Rajeev; Myers, John G.; Aaker, David A. - *Advertising Management*, Prentice Hall, 1996

(5) Binet, Les; Field, Peter – *Effectiveness in Advertising; A Manual for Brand Building*, IPA, 2018

(6) Binet, Les; Field, Peter – *The Long and the Short of It*, IPA, 2015

(7) Romaniuk, Jenni; Sharp, Byron – *How Brands Grow Part 2*, Oxford University Press, 2016

(8) Sutherland, Rory – *The Dark Art and Curious Science of Creating Magic in Brands, Business and Life*, William Morrow, 2019

(9) Halbert, Gary C. – *The Boron Letters*, Bond Halbert Publishing, 2013

(10) The Gunn report-*The link between creativity and effectiveness*, IPA, 2011 update

(11) Stephens-Davidowitz, Seth – *Everybody lies. Big data, new data, and what the internet can tell us about who we really are*, First Dey Street Books, NY, 2017

(12) Strong, Colin – *Humanizing Big Data. Marketing at the Meeting of Data, Social Science and Consumer insight*, Kogan Page Ltd, 2015

(13) Webb Young, James – *A Technique for Producing Ideas*, McGraw-Hill, 2003

(14) Binet, Les; Field, Peter – *Effectiveness in Advertising; A Manual for Brand Building*, IPA, 2018

(15) Binet, Les; Field, Peter – *The Long and the Short of It*, IPA, 2015

(16) Naples, Michael J. - *Effective frequency – The relationship between frequency and advertising effectiveness*, Association of National Advertisers, NY, 1979, pp. 59

(17) McDonald, Colin – *Advertising Reach and Frequency – Maximising Advertising Results Through Effective Frequency (2nd edition)* -NTC Business Books, 1996

(18) Flyvbjerg, Bent – *Making Social Science Matter. Why social inquiry fails and how it can succeed again*, Cambridge University Press, 2001

(19) Tiltman, David -*The anatomy of effectiveness and highlights from Cannes*, WARC, 2019

(20) Howard, John; Sheth, Jagdish – *The Theory of Buyer Behaviour*, John Wiley and Sons, 1969

(21) Steele, Jon – *Truth, Lies and Advertising- The art of account planning*, John Wiley and Sons, 1998

(22) Hoffman, Bob - *Advertising for skeptics*, Type A Group, 2020

(23) Wedel, Michel; Kamakura, Wagner – *Market Segmentation. Conceptual and Methodological Foundations Second Edition*, ISQM, Kluwer Academic Publishers, 2000

(24) https://www.alistdaily.com/lifestyle/kevin-frisch-uber-ad-fraud/

(25) https://mashable.com/2016/06/09/ad-fraud-organized-crime

(26) McDonald, Malcolm; Dunbar, Ian – *Market Segmentation – How to do it and how to profit from it – Revised 4th edition*, Wiley, 2012

(27) Sutherland, Rory -Alchemy: *The Surprising Power of Ideas That Don't Make Sense*, Virgin Digital, 2019

(28) Ritson, Mark - https://www.youtube.com/watch?v=S1xRJaNiOtU

(29) The Guardian, Oct 2, 2017

(30) Inc magazine, 2005, Sep 1

(31) Ogilvy, David - *Ogilvy on Advertising*, Vintage Books, 1985

(32) Aaker, David A - *Building Strong Brands*, Pocket Books, 2010

(33) Ambler, Tim – *Marketing and the Bottom Line*, FT Prentice Hall, 2003

(34) Taleb, Nassim Nicholas - *Fooled by Randomness: The Hidden Role of Chance in Life and in the Markets*, Cahners Business Information, 2001

(35) Batra, Rajeev; Myers, John G.; Aaker, David – *Advertising management*, Prentice Hall, 1996

(36) Sharp, Byron - *Marketing-Theory, Evidence, Practice- Second edition*, Oxford, 2017

(37) Croll, Alistair; Yoskowitz, Benjamin – *Lean Analytics. Use Data to Build a Better Startup Faster*, O'Reilly, 2013

(38) Ariely, Dan – *Predictably Irrational*, Harper Collins, 2009

(39) Ries, Eric – *The Startup Way – How Modern Companies Use Entrepreneurial Management to Transform Culture & Drive Long-Term Growth*, Currency, 2017

(40) Lord&Thomas – *The book of advertising tests: A group of articles that actually say something about advertising*, Leopold Classic Library, 2015

(41) Vakratsas, Demetrios; Ambler, Tim – *How Advertising Works: What Do We Really Know?* in Journal of Marketing, Jan 1999

(42) Just Drinks, 11 June 2020

(43) Ritson, Mark– *Elon Musk will wish he got over his hatred of advertising long ago*– Marketing Week, 11 June 2020

(44) Barta, Thomas; Barwise, Patrick – *The 12 Powers of a Marketing Leader*, McGraw-Hill, 2017

(45) Morgan, Adam- *Eating the Big Fish -How challenger brands Can Compete Against Brand Leaders*, Wiley, 2009

(46) Reeves, Rosser – *Reality in Advertising*, originally published 1961 by Alfred A. Knopf, Inc. New York, 2015

(47) Hoffman, Bob – *Laughing@advertising*, Type A Group, 2018

(48) Pringle, Hamish; Marshall, Jim- *Spending Advertising Money in the Digital Age . How to navigate the media flow*, Kogan Page. 2012

(49) Davis, John - *The Wasted Half: How to Maximize Your Advertising Dollar*

(50) Cialdini, Robert B. – *Influence- The Psychology of Persuasion*, Collins Business, 2007

(51) AdAge

(52) King, Stephen – *A Master Class in Brand Planning*, John Wiley & Sons, 2007

(53) https://edition.cnn.com/2020/07/01/tech/facebook-top-advertisers/index.html

(54) Fletcher, Winston - *Powers of Persuasion. The inside story of British advertising*, Oxford University Press, 2008

(55) https://www.msn.com/en-ca/entertainment/celebrity/ryan-reynolds-diddy-and-more-stars-with-successful-alcohol-brands/ss-BB10wejq#image=11

(56) Sharp, Byron - *How Brands Grow. What marketers don't know*, Oxford University Press, 2015

(57) Silver, Nate-*The signal and the noise. The art and science of prediction*, Pearson, 2012

(58) Rennie, Alistair; Protheroe, Jonny - *How people decide what to buy lies in the "messy middle" of the purchase journey*, July 2020

(59) https://www.fastcompany.com/3014817/amazon-jeff-bezos

(60) Dutka, Solomon-*DAGMAR. Defining Advertising Goals for Measured Advertising Results*, ANA, 1992

(61) https://customerthink.com/jan_carlzon_moments_of_truth/

(62) Hyken, Shep. *The New Moment Of Truth In Business, Forbes*. Retrieved 12 March2018.

(63) Cohen, Heidi https://heidicohen.com/marketing-the-4-moments-of-truth-chart/

(64) Solis, Brian - *Google's micro-moment of truth. Why it's a game changer for CMOs*, Forbes, April 9, 2015

(65) Lecinski, Jim - *Winning the Zero Moment of Truth* (online edition), Google, retrieved Aug 2020

(66) Edelman, David C. -*Branding in the Digital Age: You're Spending Your Money in All the Wrong Places,* Harvard Business Review, December 2010

(67) https://www.quirks.com/articles/5-founders-of-marketing-research

(68) https://www.statista.com/statistics/216573

(69) Forrester - *What Marketers Need To Know About Social Media Consumer Segmentation*, July 22, 2020

(70) Romaniuk, Jenny – *Building Distinctive Brand Assets*, Oxford University Press, 2018

(71) Barta, Thomas; Barwise, Patrick- *The 12 Powers of a Marketing Leader: How to Succeed by Building Customer and Company Value*, McGraw-Hill Education, 2016

(72) Carlzon, Jan – *Moments of Truth*, Harper Business, 1989

(73) https://www.rockefeller.edu/research/vosshall-laboratory/current-projects/completed-projects/166747-smell-study/

(74) https://thirstymag.com/slane-distillery-focus-sustainability/

(75) Webb Young, James – *How to become an advertising man*, Passport books, 1989

(76) Martineau, Pierre – *Motivation for Advertising*, Mc Graw-Hill, 1971

(77) Bernbach, Bill – *Bill Bernbach said*, DDB Needham Wroldwide, 1989

APPENDIX 1: MARKETING EFFECTIVENESS TEST

ORGANIZATION

1. **Which of the following statements best describes your organization's process for marketing effectiveness:**

Marketing activation and assessment done in siloed teams (at brand and/or channel level)

Relevant channel partners collaborate for important campaigns, few times per year, but weekly interaction is limited

Clear cross-channel processes and ways of working across channel roles and external agencies

Fully integrated and agile ways of working across channel teams and with external agencies

2. **Which of the following best describes how your agency partners work together:**

Agencies work mostly independently

Some cross-agency collaboration, especially if their work is complimentary

Cross-agency collaboration, with regular all-agency meetings (e.g. for campaign planning)

All agencies collaborate actively

3. How are the objectives/KPIs of your marketing activities set?

Independent objectives by channel

Largely independent objectives by channel, with some common objectives

Common objectives across multiple channels (ex: across all digital channels, but not between digital and experiential)

Common objectives across all digital and non-digital channels

4. Do you benchmark the cost of marketing departments between different affiliates/markets

No

We benchmark 1 or 2 elements (# of FTE vs size of business, # of FTE/A&P, cost of the marketing department as % of total structure cost, # of layers in the organization)

We benchmark (almost) all of the above elements

PROMOTIONS

"Sales promotion is a range of tactical marketing techniques designed within a strategic framework in order to achieve specific sales and marketing objectives" – The Institute of Sales Promotion

1. Within your organization, do you have dedicated people measuring the effectiveness of your promotions (ex: Revenue Growth Managers calculating ROIs for promotions)?

No

Yes, but not fully dedicated

Yes, fully dedicated resource(s)

2. Within your organization, which of the following you think represent the core issues when doing sales promotions (multiple choice possible):

Increase Volume

Increase Trial

Increase repeat purchase

Increase loyalty

Widening usage

Creating interest

Creating awareness

Deflecting attention from price

Rewarding loyal consumers

I do not know/ I am not sure

3. **Within your organization, how many of the following core objectives for sales promotions do you usually define (multiple choice possible):**

Increase Volume

Increase Trial

Increase repeat purchase

Increase loyalty

Widening usage

Creating interest

Creating awareness

Deflecting attention from price

Rewarding loyal consumers

I do not know/ I am not sure

4. Within your organization, did you define a set of "golden rules" regarding the ideal promotions by channel (i.e. length of the promotion, depth of discount, frequency of promotions, the period of promo by category, seasonality, etc.)

No

We have a few rules, but they are not exhaustive and are mostly empirical

Yes, we do have a set of comprehensive rules, but they are not updated regularly

Yes, we do have a set of rules that are updated regularly

5. Within your organization, what is the % of sales in e-commerce as a % of total sales?

Less than 1%

Between 1 and 5%

Between 5% and 10%

Bigger than 10%

PRICE MANAGEMENT

"The single most important decision in evaluating a business is pricing power" – Warren Buffett

1. In your organization, how do you do your price positioning?

Price index vs main competitors decided centrally

Cost-plus, regardless of competitor positioning

Value pricing (willingness of the consumer to pay)

Price index vs competition decided at local level

2. In your organization, how often do you analyze your price vs your main competitors?

Every month or every two months

Every week

Every day

We monitor price less than once every 2 months

3. In your organization, do you do regular price elasticity assessments?

I do not remember last time we did it

Yes, we do some correlations internally (a posteriori regression analysis using historical data) between price and sales or market share in some channels

Yes, we do regular research using direct questions to consumers (Van Westendorp, Gabor Granger,…)

Yes, we do regular pricing studies using conjoint analysis to optimize different business levers (sales, volumes, market share, profit)

We use expert opinion (ex: Pricestrat, MaxDiff)

4. **In your opinion, have you fully exploited the willingness to pay of the consumer for your products?**

Not really

Yes, we are not so bad

Yes, we are better than the competition

I do not know

5. **In your opinion, to which extent can you fulfil next year value creation targets with pricing initiatives?**

Not at all, no pricing power in my market (pricing power below inflation)

Some pricing power, but below what is expected by management (more or less inflation)

Good pricing power, better than inflation

I do not know

CREATIVITY & INNOVATION

1. **On a scale of 1 to 10, how would you rate the creativity of your campaigns vs your main competitors?**

Your company   1 2 3 4 5 6 7 8 9 10
Main Competitor 1   ....   1 2 3 4 5 6 7 8 9 10
Main Competitor 2   ....   1 2 3 4 5 6 7 8 9 10
Main Competitor 3   ....   1 2 3 4 5 6 7 8 9 10

2. **What kind of research you do to test your creativity?** (multiple choice possible)

Live testing (incl A/B testing)

Qual (ex : focus groups)

Online quant

Neuroscience

None of the above

3. **On a scale from 1 to 10, how would you rate you're the consistency of your advertising message vs your main competitors?**

Your company   1 2 3 4 5 6 7 8 9 10
Main Competitor 1   ....   1 2 3 4 5 6 7 8 9 10
Main Competitor 2   ....   1 2 3 4 5 6 7 8 9 10
Main Competitor 3   ....   1 2 3 4 5 6 7 8 9 10

4. **What is the % of innovations in your total sales ?**

………….%

5. **How does the % of innovations in your total sales compare with your main competitors?**

Pretty much the same

We have a higher % of innovations than the competition

We have a lower % of innovations than the competition

6. **How do you manage hosting of your creatives?**

Some creatives are hosted on an online ad platform

All static creatives are hosted on an online ad platform

All static creatives hosted on an online ad platform, including some dynamic creatives

7. **To what extent have you automated your creative process for digital?**

Ads are created manually and optimized manually

We create most ads manually and use standard platform features like creative rotation. Effectiveness optimized manually

We use dynamic creatives using mostly data feeds. We use both manual and automated optimization

8. **Which of the following best describes how you set up and manage your campaigns?**

All campaign setup and management done by an external agency

We mainly use the existing ad platform user interface to setup and manage our campaigns

We use the platform user interface but also leverage APIs for campaign setup and reporting

We make heavy use of platform APIs and structured data files for campaign setup and reporting

9. **Which of the following tracking methodologies do you use (multiple choice possible)**

Brand tracking

Consumer surveys

Marketing mix modelling (econometrics)

Controlled experiments

Other methodologies (specify)

10. **Does your organization or your agency have a consistent web analytics suite?**

No

Yes, the agency has

Yes, we have one internally

Yes, operated by us and connected to other systems (ex: demand side platform)

11. To which extent is your organization using data and benchmarking to inform creative development?

Creatives are based only on brand principles/brand compass

Creatives are based mainly on insights from a specific channel and analytics

Creatives are based on insights from all relevant channels and analytics

PACKAGING

1. On a scale of 1 to 10, how would you rate the packaging of your brands vs your main competitors?

Your company	1 2 3 4 5 6 7 8 9 10
Main Competitor 1	1 2 3 4 5 6 7 8 9 10
Main Competitor 2	1 2 3 4 5 6 7 8 9 10
Main Competitor 3	1 2 3 4 5 6 7 8 9 10

2. What kind of research you do to test your packaging? (multiple choice possible)

Live testing

Qual (ex: focus groups)

Online quant

Other

None of the above

3. **Do you know how important packaging is in the marketing mix?**

Yes, it is very important

Yes, it is not very important

No, it is not so important

We do not know

TARGETING

1. **Within your organization, do you have channel specialists (e.g. search, social, programmatic) that support digital marketing function?**

No

Yes, but not fully dedicated

Yes, fully dedicated resource

2. How do you buy digital media?

We mainly buy directly from publishers (reservation) or from ad networks

We mainly buy programmatic

None of the above

3. What is your digital display marketing strategy?

We mainly buy desktop display and video

We buy display and video across desktop and mobile; we follow an audience strategy for each within channel and format

We buy across all relevant channels and formats . We apply audience and targeting strategies across all channels and formats

None of the above

4. What sources of insights do you use to build your audiences for email campaigns?

We rely mainly on 3rd party data, provided by platforms we advertise on

We use 3rd party and 1st party data from digital channel

We use 3rd party and 1st party data, from both online and offline channel

None of the above

5. **How do you connect systems to get insights from data in order to improve marketing activation?**

Limited connectivity, data used independently by channel

Connectivity in online channels

Online and offline systems connected

6. **Does your organization use a CRM suite?**

No

Yes, it is operated by an external agency

Yes, it is operated by us

Yes, it is operated by us and connected to other systems (ex: DMP)

7. **Does your organization use tailoring for audience messaging in email?**

No, same message send to all

Messages tailored by broad type of segments

Messages tailored to all available segments

8. **Does your organization use a DMP (Data management Platform)?**

No

Yes, it is operated by an external agency

Yes, it is operated by us

Yes, it is operated by us and connected to other systems (ex: CRM)

9. Do you have a clear segmentation of your consumers?

Yes, based mainly on demographics

Yes, based on demographics and lifestyle

Yes, based on demographics, lifestyle and behavior

No

10. Have you identified the needs and uses/occasions for which consumers buy your products?

Yes, we have identified the main needs, but not for all categories

Yes, we have identified the main needs for all categories

No/ I do not know

COMM PLANNING

1. Which of the following performance metrics do you use to assess your marketing effectiveness? (multiple choice possible)

Campaign metrics (ex: cost per click, cost per contact, CPM)

Conversion metrics (ex: number of conversions, footfall, opportunities to see)

Revenue or profitability metrics (ex: ROI)

Effective reach

Influential reach

None of the above

2. How would you describe the feedback mechanisms you have in place to measure your marketing activations?

Limited test and learn. Results influence annual planning

Regular use of testing. Results influence next campaign

Always-on testing. Results influence campaigns while they are running

3. How would you describe the connection between your touchpoints?

Our communication channels /touchpoints are run largely independently

Our communication channels/touchpoints are coordinated, without a shared timeline

Our communication channels/touchpoints are coordinated, with a shared timeline

4. What is your A&P split by touchpoint (in %)?

Digital media …..

Traditional media….

Search …..

Experiential/events …..

PR/ Influencers ……

POS …..

VAP …..

Sponsorship….

Displays and other last 3 feet …..

Research ….

Other…..

5. Do you keep track of your touchpoint costs and their evolution?

Yes

Only for some of them

None of them

6. **Do you benchmark your touchpoint costs between different affiliates?**

Yes

No

7. **Do you measure the reach of each of your touchpoints?**

No

Yes, but only a few of them

Yes, all of them

8. **Do you measure the comparative impact on consumers of each of your touchpoints?**

No

Yes, but only a few of them

Yes, all of them

PORTFOLIO MANAGEMENT

1. **Have you identified a consumer demand map (consumer segments vs needs and occasions) for each of your categories you compete?**

Yes

No

2. Have you identified a role for each brand in your portfolio (ex: Fighter, Support/Flanker,...)?

Yes

No

3. Have you identified specific competitors in each consumer need/occasion?

Yes

No

4. Have you identified/prioritized requirements to win in each consumer need/occasion?

Yes

No

STRATEGY AND RESOURCE ALLOCATION

1. Do you have a strategic framework for brand investment depending on brand strategic role (ex: Growth Relay, Bastion, Star, ...)

Yes

No

2. **Do you have a strategic framework for brand investment depending on their respective ROI?**

Yes

No

3. **Do you have a strategic framework for brand investment depending on market maturity/product life cycle?**

Yes

No

4. **Do you have a strategic framework for market investment depending on market potential?**

Yes

No

5. **Do you have a single source of truth for your consumer researches, that markets and agencies can have access to?**

Yes

No

6. How would you rate your ability to create case studies/ business cases?

We do not do case studies/business cases

We are pretty good

We are excellent

7. How often do you do best practice sharing within your company? Between affiliates?

Every month

Every quarter

Every 6 months

Once per year

COMPETITIVE ASSESSMENT

1. How do you measure your Share of Voice vs the competition?

- We monitor their spend by touchpoint by week or month

- We monitor their spend by touchpoint every 6 months or once per year

- We monitor their investments by touchpoint by channel by week or month

- We monitor their investments by touchpoint by channel every 6 months or once per year

2. How do you measure your Share of Market vs the competition?

–   We monitor our share in volume and value by channel by week or month

–   We monitor our share in volume and value by channel every quarter or less often

–   We monitor our share in volume and value, only in some channels, by week or month

–   We monitor our share in volume and value, only in some channels, every 6 months or once per year

3. How do you measure your performance by touchpoint vs the competition?

We do not measure performance by touchpoint vs competition

We do measure performance by touchpoint vs competition, every 3 months or more often

We do measure performance by touchpoint vs competition, every 6 months or less often

4. How often do you assess market trends in your industry?

We do not asses trends in our industry on a regular basis

We do asses trends in our industry on a regular basis, every 3 months or more often

We do asses trends in our industry on a regular basis, every 6 months or less often

APPENDIX 2. SOME HISTORIC BUYERS AND CREATORS OF CRAFT BRANDS

<u>Whiskies</u>

Slane Irish whisky – bought by **Brown Forman**

https://www.slaneirishwhiskey.com/

Lambay Irish whiskey – created by **Camus**

https://www.lambaywhiskey.com/

Westland Distillery (Washington)– bought by **Remy Cointreau**

https://westlanddistillery.com/

Wyoming whiskey- strategic partnership with **Edrington**

https://www.wyomingwhiskey.com/

High West (Utah) - bought by **Constellation Brands**

https://www.highwest.com/

Smooth Ambler (West Virginia) – bought by **Pernod Ricard**

https://smoothambler.com/

Gins

Malfy gin (Italy) – bought by **Pernod Ricard**

https://www.malfygin.com/

Monkey 47 (Germany) – bought by **Pernod Ricard**

https://monkey47.com/

Inverroche (South Africa)– bought by **Pernod Ricard**

https://www.inverroche.com/za/

KI NO BI (Japan) – bought by **Pernod Ricard**

https://kyotodistillery.jp/en-GB/products/kinobi/

Bulldog (UK) – bought by **Campari Group**

http://www.bulldoggin.com/v2/

Sipsmith (UK) – bought by **Beam Suntory**

Gin Sul – bought by **Mast Jägermeister**

Fords – bought by **Brown Forman**

Aviation American Gin – bought by **Diageo** for US$610m

https://www.aviationgin.com/

Beer

Ballast Point – bought by Constellation Brands in 2015 for 1Bn USD and sold to Kings & Convicts Brewing Co. in 2019.

https://ballastpoint.com/

Blue Moon (US) – bought by Miller Coors

Goose Island (US) – bought by **Anheuser Busch**

Leinenkugel's (US) - bought by **Miller**

Unibroue (US)- bought by **Sapporo**

ABOUT THE AUTHOR

Corneliu Vilsan

I have enjoyed 20 years as a CEO and Marketing practitioner, living and working across the globe, in many different categories (body and hair care, children toiletries, sanitary protection, and spirits and wine). My last position as a marketing practitioner was as CMO of Pernod Ricard EMEA-LATAM, after which I decided to open my own strategic marketing consultancy called EFF-E Marketing, based in Paris.

During my career, I met hundreds of marketers, and the most successful ones were those who were curious and eager to learn how markets and advertising operate, what drives consumer choice and how to increase the odds of delivering the strategic objectives of the company. This quest for understanding made the difference between those who advanced in their career and those who did not. I am still fascinated by how much it is still to be discovered and how much I can continue to learn in the marketing field, and I want to share in this book some of the secrets I learned during my career.

Fabiana Vilsan helped me wrote the Digital chapter. She graduated with Magna Cum Laude from Brown University and has worked as Analyst, Account Director and Marketing Director for a variety of technology companies based in the US.